The Jewish Vote

Obama vs. Romney:
A Jewish Voter's Guide

By Shmuel Rosner

Contents

Cover Design by Jonathan Fong

Prologue: Why 2012 (Jewishly) Matters

2008 was a no-brainer.

Yes, for a couple of months there was noise, there was a shadow, there was doubt. There were people spreading the rumor that things might be changing. I plead guilty to being one of them — not the worst, but I did my share. In retrospect though, it is clear that Barack Obama versus John McCain was a no-brainer. There was no way that a vast number of Jewish voters would suddenly flock to the Republican camp after close to a hundred years of loyalty. There was no way that Jewish voters would not stay on the wagon edging toward as exciting a destination as the election of the first black president. There was no way that a large number of Jewish voters would toss away the promise of hope and change to cast their vote for George W. Bush's Republican successor. All Obama had to do was pass a couple of simple tests to get his fair share of the Jewish vote. Three out of every four Jews voted for him. In New York and California, in New Jersey and Florida, in Ohio and Pennsylvania.

2004 was a no-brainer.

It was hardly as exciting as the 2008 campaign, and hardly as historic: the Democratic candidate had a wooden quality to him, and Republicans were viciously attacking him, and the incumbent was one of Israel's best friends in the White House ever. But truly, when the war in Iraq was the issue of the day — a war to which most Jews were opposed from day one[1] — there was not a chance that Bush would get a share of the Jewish vote much higher than what Republicans had gotten used to from Jewish voters since the early 90's.

2000 was a no-brainer.

With Joe Lieberman, the first Jewish candidate of a major party for the vice presidency? With a candidate who had been the vice president of Bill Clinton, beloved by the Jews, a staunch friend of Israel? Jewish voters had no doubt: the Gore-Lieberman ticket was the Jewish ticket. Ninety percent of them "approved" of Al Gore's selection of Lieberman.[2] About 80 percent ended up voting for the Democratic ticket — it was the third presidential round in a row for Jews to vote with almost the exact same majority for the Democratic ticket: 77 percent for Clinton in 1992, 79 percent for Clinton in 1996, 79 percent for Gore in 2000[3] (John Kerry got 77 percent, and Obama 74 percent of the vote respectively in 2004 and 2008). "In eight of the ten presidential cycles between 1972 and 2008 the Democratic presidential nominee ran between 22 and 32 points better among Jewish American voters than he did among all American voters."[4] And it is no wonder that the gap between Jews and non-Jews reached its peak in 2000, when Lieberman was on the ticket.

Will 2012 be any different? Can it be any different?

Consider this: 2012 will mark the 20-year anniversary of a new era in American Jewish politics-- the Republican-Party-is-not-an-option-for-most-Jews era. 2012 will also mark the 10-year anniversary of another new era in American Jewish politics: the Israel-as-wedge-issue era. These two trends of Jewish voting are interconnected in many ways, some simple and easily visible to the public, some more nuanced and out of sight. To understand the special significance of 2012, one has to unearth the meaning beyond these two anniversaries.

* * *

Why Jews, for the last 20 years, have voted for Democratic candidates in such great numbers is a question that will be investigated mainly in chapters two and three of this book. But something has to be said now: Two processes began much earlier culminated in the early 90's, and both pulled most Jewish voters ever closer to the Democratic Party and pushed them away from the Republican Party.

One process was internal to a Jewish Americanism that was becoming less tribal and more universalist, less apprehensive and more confident, less defensive and more affluent. And as these trends were changing the face of American Judaism, they also made many Jews more inclined to identify their Judaism with liberal ideals, to mix them together in ways that made them at times indistinguishable from one another.

The other, second, process was external to the Jewish community and involved changes in the nature of both the Democratic and the Republican parties. The Democratic Party, after many years, was finally able to get rid of the tradition of leftist radicalism that had haunted it from the 1968 Chicago convention, moving through to the McGovern candidacy and defeat of 1972, to the Carter presidency of 1976 and defeat of 1980, and to the miserable candidacies of Walter Mondale (1984) and Michael Dukakis (1988). In Bill Clinton, the party had finally found its way back to the center. Liberal enough on domestic issues, without being suspiciously defeatist on foreign policy. Responsible enough on economic issues, without an abandonment of the language of compassion and empathy.

And while the Democrats were moving back to the political center, the Republicans were becoming less centrist — less dominated by an established group of elitist patriarchs — and more the party of the heartland. The Barry Goldwater insurgency of the 60's, the Ronald Reagan presidency of the 80's, were now turning into a sense of ownership. The Huns — religious devotees, flat tax radicals, gun rights purists, state rights advocates, anti-abortion street fighters, war-on-Christmas alarmists, radio show populists — were taking over the party. And if not quite taking over — as the Romney

nomination and the 1996 Bob Dole nomination prove —
then taking over its image, especially among Jews.

Jewish Americans have been part of the Democratic
coalition since the Franklin Roosevelt years. However —
as we will demonstrate in greater detail later — they felt
even more comfortable and much less troubled in the
reinvented Democratic Party, and felt very
uncomfortable with the reinvented Republican Party.
When Democrats no longer had McGoverns and Carters
to abandon, and Republicans no longer had Eisenhowers
to consider, the choice became a no-choice — the no-
brainers that were 2000 and 2004 and 2008.

But as I said a few paragraphs ago, the 2012 elections
will not only mark the 20-year anniversary of the
Republican-Party-is-not-an-option era. It will also mark
the 10-year anniversary of the Israel-as-wedge-issue era.
Since 2002, and more ferociously in the 2004 and 2008
presidential cycles and the 2006 and 2010 midterm
cycles, the Republicans have been making the case that
voting for a Democrat is voting against Israel. This is not
an entirely new argument. Proponents of Richard Nixon
used it in 1972, when George McGovern was on the
other side, and it definitely played a role in the Carter-
Reagan election of 1980.

However, in past cycles the Republicans would have had
the incentive to use this line of argument only when the
Democrats selected a nominee who could be easily
portrayed as problematic to Israel because of prior

statements (George McGovern) or prior actions (Jimmy Carter) — and only when the Republican candidate was not himself suspect on Israel-related matters. They could not use it against Clinton in 1992, when George H. W. Bush and his secretary of state, James Baker, seemed to many much more unsympathetic toward Israel than the very sympathetic Democratic duo of Clinton and Gore. And they could certainly not use it when the son of Bush, the still relatively unknown George W. Bush, was running against Gore and Lieberman.

Two things changed the past dynamic and replaced it with the constant campaign of the Republicans-are-better-for-Israel argument. The first is the change that we've mentioned within the Republican Party. This change, and the religious and ideological tendencies of many of the party's voters, have eliminated — at least for the time being — any chance of nomination for a candidate who is not staunchly and demonstrably friendly toward Israel. However, the second change is no less significant. That's the change in the outlook of the U.S. on the Middle East. The attacks of 9/11, the wars in Afghanistan and Iraq, the so-called war on terror that, rhetoric aside, continues under President Obama. The U.S., starting in 2001, ceased looking at the Middle East almost solely through its traditional peace process lens. And while some American notables still believe that the Israeli-Arab peace process is key to solving other Middle East problems, most others realize by now that this region is much too complicated to be calmed by peace agreements between Israel and its neighbors.

Israel's strategic situation has also changed, quite dramatically. If the 90's gave some the impression, or the false hope, that the end of this chapter in history was near — that is, in Israel's case, an end to hostilities between Israel and its enemies — the next decade was an eye-opener. Beginning with the collapse of the Israeli-Palestinian peace process in 2000 (still under Clinton), and including the eruption of the second Palestinian Intifada, the rise of Hamas and Hezbollah, the Second Lebanon War, and, more than all of these, the looming threat of a nuclearized Iran — events have made Israel more apprehensive, and those who care about Israel more persistent in making it a priority.

And these two changes — Republicans drawing closer to Israel, and dangers drawing closer to Israel — were the reason for the 10-year span of Israel being the wedge issue. The reason — and the tool. Republicans have been trying to use these new realities, political and strategic, to rally Jewish voters and Jewish donors (with the side benefit of rallying Zionist evangelicals using the same message). For 10 years now, they have attempted to argue that a vote for a candidate of the Democratic Party — a Kerry or an Obama, or many other candidates for the House, Senate, and local elections — is a vote that endangers Israel.

Twenty years of fewer Jews voting for Republican candidates. Ten years of the Republican Party's attempting to turn the tide by using the Israel card. And we are fast approaching 2012.

* * *

Delving deeper into American Jewish political behavior, one finds an interesting parallel between the tactics of the two parties. In a way, both parties have the same goal in mind: to change the topic of conversation. Republicans want to constantly talk about how good their party is on Israel, and how bad Democrats can be. Democrats want to constantly talk about how bad Republicans are on domestic social issues, and how bad they can be on church-state issues, given the growing evangelical influence within the party. Republicans would like to make Israel the issue; Democrats want to neutralize Israel as an issue. Democrats would like to make health care and abortion the issue; Republicans want to make them secondary to more urgent issues at hand (such as the economy and Iran).

Of course, many Jewish voters go to the polls thinking about politics without even considering the "Jewish" angle; for many of them, voting has no distinctly Jewish angle. They are liberal and vote for the Democrats, or conservative and vote for the Republicans, for whatever political considerations. However, for those tending to incorporate their Jewish sentiment into this broader calculation of voting preferences, the debate between the Obama Jewish camp and the Romney Jewish camp is not just a tactical debate of presidential politics. It is also a debate that is reflective of internal dynamics within American Judaism, a debate that is a little challenging to accurately describe, as no brief description can capture all the elements that go through each citizen's mind as he or she enters the voting booth.

Using a very broad brush, I'd paint the competition between Jewish Democrats and Jewish Republicans as one between a more utopian Judaism and a more hard-nosed Judaism.

On the one side, there is the majority of Democratic Jews (that is, the majority of Jews) — those wanting to focus first and foremost on "Jewish ideals," broadly defined as universal humanistic values. These ideals are what make Judaism appealing to many American Jews in this era of religious freedom and in an open market of religions. In many instances, "ideals" make it easier for Jews to keep their Jewish identity without having to commit themselves to specific practices and particularistic (or tribal) behaviors.

The Democratic case for making Jewish ideals the core of Jewish political conduct is an appealing one for a generation of young Jews who pursue a Judaism that is "more personal, more informal, more episodic" than the previous generation.[5] For such a generation, voting for the Democratic Party (75–80 percent of Jews) is a ritual — similar to attending a Passover Seder (80 percent of Jewish college students[6]), fasting on Yom Kippur (81 percent for unmarried young Jewish couples with children[7]); a little less common than lighting Hanukah candles (90 percent of college students[8]); and much more than having a mezzuzah on one's door (61 percent of all Jews[9]), lighting Shabbat candles (just 23 percent of the more Jewishly engaged), or keeping kosher at home (17 percent of the Jewishly connected).

Competing with this vision of Jewish ideals is the vision of a sterner Judaism. A Judaism that is more concerned with traditional Jewish practice, Jewish physical survival, Jewish interests, and is less concerned about bringing Judaism in line with the new religion of humanistic values (as interpreted by the modern priests of humanistic religion — namely, university professors and "tikkun olam" activists).

Of course, Jewish Republicans have as many ideals as Jewish Democrats; they are concerned with values as much as Jewish Democrats, but for them, voting for a certain party is not like lighting candles: it is a political deed, not a religious one. It is quite ironic, then, that the growing Jewish Republican camp is based, to a large extent, on the growing Orthodox sector. Contrary to what is customarily seen as the over-mixing of politics and religion by the more traditional sections of society, the Jews have it backward: the more liberal — and, generally speaking, less traditional — treat their vote more religiously. The more conservative — and, generally speaking, more traditional — treat their political preferences more secularly.

Broad brush — as there are many holes in this theory and many nuances missed in such a description of American Jewish reality. This is not to say that Democrats don't necessarily care as much about practical solutions for America or that Jewish Republicans don't care as much about their different interpretation of Jewish ideals. Or indeed that Democrats' practice of Judaism is of less worth or that the Republican agenda is against humanistic values. And naturally, many voters, if not most, are somewhere in the middle, at times utopian, at times more hard-nosed. But this is the divide many of them are straddling. So save all (justified) reservations for later, and just look at this attempt at painting a broad picture. Now think: Jews for Obama versus Jews for Romney. Does it fit?

* * *

The 2012 election has no chance of being as exciting as the 2008 election (although it could turn out to be a much more competitive nail-biter). From a Jewish perspective, this election also has no chance of being as exhilarating as the one in 2000. But it will present Jewish voters with an interesting choice at this double anniversary of Jews' flocking to support Democratic candidates overwhelmingly, and of Jews' being wooed by a constant Republican claim that the GOP is the better party for Israel. It will be interesting because many of the factors that made 2008, 2004 and 2000 no-brainer elections are gone. There's no Jewish candidate on the list, no first African American candidate to support, no unpopular Bush to get rid of, no underlining of religious skirmishes. In Obama, the Democratic Party has a candidate who is still well-liked but also battle-scarred. In 2012, one must pick Obama for his philosophy, for his actions and for his performance in office, not for symbolic reasons that supersede all political calculations. And the Republican Party is proposing as an alternative a candidate who made his career (and fortune) by being a pragmatist. A religious man, he does not claim to be guided by God. A conservative man, he had no qualms as governor of Massachusetts about working with Democrats and putting forward programs in step with Democratic ideas.

We know that in the course of the campaign, Obama will attempt to rekindle the passion voters felt for him four years ago; we know that in the course of the campaign, Romney will be forced to maneuver carefully to avoid the wrath of conservative voters. But we also know that, campaign propaganda aside, the two candidates standing for election are much more grounded than their images may indicate. Obama is not a messiah, Romney is not a radical; Obama is not a bipartisan uniter, Romney is not a partisan divider; Obama is not an enemy of Israel, Romney is not a trigger-happy warmonger.

In 2012, for the first time in many years, Jewish voters — if they wish to — can look at the candidates without much emotion, without much fanfare. It was commonly agreed by many commentators that Romney's selection of Paul Ryan as his running mate makes this election more about ideas — more dispassionate debate about numbers and the economy and governing philosophies, rather than about the personality of the candidates and the gaffes and the other silly stuff that elections are always filled with. Jewish voters also get a chance to be somewhat less passionate about their choice. Obama, as all should agree, is not as exciting today as he was four years ago. And Romney, with his wooden, robotic posture, is also not the most exciting Republican candidate of recent decades.

Thus, 2012 is significant for its lack of great passion, for the gravity of a choice between two imperfect candidates: Which of the two is better prepared to dispassionately handle a struggling economy? Which of the two better understands the risk of a nuclearized Iran and is better equipped to deal with it? Which of the two is ready to tackle America's national problems without imposing on them unrealistic, ideological solutions?

This guide is about the Jewish vote and Jewish voters. It is bipartisan by conscious decision and will not attempt to tell you who to vote for. Nor will it tell you who the author thinks is the better choice. It will focus on issues that are markedly "Jewish" and on the story of two parties and two candidates attempting to woo the Jewish vote, trying to overcome Jewish suspicion and reservations, looking for ways to resonate with Jewish themes. Jewish voters — like all other American voters — have only one vote, but that vote is the only vote that is also Jewish. And this makes it remarkably interesting, and very special. To know why, keep reading.

Shmuel Rosner, September 2012.

1. Why Jews Matter

Friday morning, December 30, just 24 hours before the end of 2011, and I was freezing. It was windy, it was wet, and with the windchill factor, it felt like 24 degrees. It *was* 24 degrees. Surrounded by hundreds of excited Iowa voters, I was bemoaning the political enthusiasm of these good citizens. If only fewer of them had shown up to see presidential candidate Mitt Romney, this rally would have taken place inside the warm grocery store, as was originally planned. But due to the unexpected crowds, they had to take it outside, and Romney could tell us all that "we're out in the cold and the rain and the wind because we care about America" while President Obama was playing golf in Hawaii. Obama was on a vacation at the time, and Hawaii did seem like a very good idea on that Iowa morning. Of course, Mr. and Mrs. Romney had just started the long journey that they hoped would lead them to the White House — a good enough reason to suffer a little cold — but what were the rest of us doing there?

Four years earlier, following Obama and the other 2008 candidates on the campaign trail, I heard Obama's rival, John McCain, the eventual Republican nominee, repeating a joke both in Iowa and later in New Hampshire.[10] It is really a quote of a joke once told by the late U.S. Representative Morris (Mo) Udall, a 1976 presidential candidate. Udall was a Mormon candidate, like Romney, but unlike Romney — at least in public — he was also a funny man. In McCain's creaky version, the joke went like this: "One New Hampshire man asks another what he thinks of Udall. The second man replies, 'I don't know. I've only met him twice.'"

A second of hesitation always followed McCain's telling of the joke, and then came the chuckle. No big laughs, just a chuckle. We got it: The voters in Iowa and New Hampshire are spoiled. They want to meet their candidates more than once or twice, and not just via the television. They want to know as much as possible about them. They take their role as the first to cast their ballots seriously, a role that many believe it is high time someone took from them.

There are other indications as to how seriously Iowa voters take their role: In the 2004 election cycle, one out of every five Democratic voters in Iowa decided for whom they would cast their vote in the last three days leading up to the caucuses. This is a measure of Iowa voters' earnestness. They don't just make up their minds based on tradition or prejudice; they look into the matter up until the last minute. That's why, regardless of the wind chill factor, Iowa is the place to be on the eve of a caucus for those who love politics.

True, its voters might not always pick the winner: many candidates have succeeded in winning the race even though they lost in Iowa — like Republican President Ronald Reagan, who lost in Iowa to George H.W. Bush in 1980. And many have not won the race even though they won in Iowa — like Mike Huckabee in 2008 and Rick Santorum in 2012.[11]

But Iowa's importance, derived from being a first in the nation primary state, is still undeniable. It played a decisive role when Jimmy Carter won the candidacy in 1976; it also did so in 2004, when it buried what seemed to be the surefire candidacy of Howard Dean; and it anointed the two who would represent the Democratic Party — John Kerry and John Edwards. George W. Bush was also victorious in Iowa in 2000. But even in years such as 1988, when Iowa's candidates were Democrat Richard Gephardt and Republican Robert Dole, Iowans' sense of self-importance is always palpable. Like it or not, they project an image of bellwether voters.

So politicians flock to Iowa. Journalists follow on their tracks. They may determine nothing — after all, Iowa's 25 delegates represent about 1 percent of the total number of delegates in the Republican convention. Such a tiny fracture. And yet such an inflated sense of importance that it actually becomes a reality.

In this they remind me of the Jews.

* * *

No one really knows exactly how many Jews there are in the United States: too few to be reliably polled, too confusingly defined to be reliably counted. In the largest study of the American Jewish community of recent decades, the number was estimated to be around 5.2 million.[12] Yet later studies repudiated that figure, setting the number higher — at 6.4 million [13] (a Brandeis University team) or closer to 6.6 million (Ira Sheskin of Miami University and Arnold Dashefsky of Connecticut University[14]). Of course, not all Jews vote, but they do historically vote at a much higher rate than the rest of the American public, and the Jewish population is older than the rest of the general public. In other words, more Jews, possibly close to 80 percent, are eligible to vote. That's 80 percent of the approximately 2 percent of Americans who are Jewish, of which many go to the polls come Election Day, adding up to maybe as many as five million Jewish voters across the country.[15]

Jews tend to move to states with a high number of electoral votes: The "top four states with the largest Jewish populations account for 127 electoral votes"; the "top 10 states with the largest Jewish populations account for 244 electoral votes." However, most Jews cast their ballots in places where there will be no real competition between Obama and Romney. Four states account for more than half of all American Jews: New York,[16] California, Florida and New Jersey. Eight states have a population of close to a quarter of a million Jews: New York, California, Florida, New Jersey, Illinois, Pennsylvania, Massachusetts, Maryland. In New York, Jews make up about 8 percent of the population. In New Jersey it is 5–6 percent. In Maryland and Massachusetts the percentage is also greater than 4 percent.[17]

However, most of these states are not expected to be battlefield states. President Obama is going to cruise to victory in most of them without having to invest much time campaigning, whether among Jews or non-Jews. The notable exception is Florida, a toss-up state, and a must-win for Romney, in which Jews make about 3.5 percent of the population. Pennsylvania (2.3 percent Jewish) is a less probable exception — a state in which Romney is making an investment but not a state that the Jews could reasonably deliver even if the vote were very close. The McCain campaign of 2008 also hoped for a while to take Pennsylvania but didn't even come close.[18] New Jersey is even less probable: it went for the Republican candidate from 1972 to 1988, but for the Democratic candidate ever since. Nevertheless, in almost every election cycle there's a point at which Republicans flirt with the idea of a New Jersey win.

Florida and maybe, just maybe, Ohio, Pennsylvania and New Jersey — with so few Jews in so few states of consequence, one wonders: does the Jewish vote even matter? "With most elections being decided by 1–5 percentage points, even a small minority can influence an election, particularly in states with somewhat larger percentages of Jews," declares one researcher.[19] "The Jewish seniors in South Florida always have disproportionate influence in an election year," points out another writer.[20] Others are more skeptical. In reality, for Jewish votes to be of any significance come Election Day, the margin between candidates has to be very small — very, very small — and in very specific areas.[21]

Take Ohio for example. Jews in this state comprise 1.3 percent of the population and about 3 percent of the vote. In 2004, a very close election, George W. Bush took the state by 2.1 percent of the entire Ohio electorate. This means that even in the tightest of elections, you need every single Jew to vote as one bloc to make a difference. That is very unlikely to happen, as even the most optimistic (among Republican operatives) and the most pessimistic (among Democratic operatives) put the percentage of Jewish swing voters in play at no higher than 15 percent, which could potentially be added to the 24 percent of Jewish Americans who voted for John McCain in 2008.

Or take Florida, the most talked-about state of possible Jewish consequence, a state in which the Jews were allegedly responsible for a month-long lock on the presidential pick following the 2000 elections, a state where Joe Lieberman was able to bring Al Gore very close to winning, thanks to, among others, Jewish voters. Florida has been, for a number of years now, the ground zero of American Jewish politics — from Lieberman of 2000 to the Sarah Silverman video supporting Obama of 2008.

Lieberman is the most demonstrable manifestation to date of American Jewish political prowess, having been the Democratic VP candidate. But in 2008 Lieberman was in Florida to support his good friend, Senator McCain (McCain would later even consider him as possible running mate). When I saw Lieberman there, trying to convince Jewish residents of the state, many of whom are of retirement age, to vote for the Republican candidate,[22] I was reminded of an old story about the 1952 Adlai Stevenson campaign. When Stevenson was campaigning in California — or so the story goes[23] — a woman asked him where he got his tan. "You been playing golf?" the woman asked. "No," responded Stevenson, "I got this tan making outdoor speeches in Florida." "Well," said the woman, "if you got that brown, you talked for too long."

Thus, in 2008 Florida, while Obama was struggling to convince Jewish voters that he would provide firm support for Israel, Lieberman talked too long about why the opposite was true. He told them that Obama's Mideast policy was going to hurt Israel and the United States. Following an Obama address to the pro-Israel lobby AIPAC, reporters were called in to see Lieberman. "I appreciate many of the very good intentions toward Israel that Senator Obama expressed today," the Jewish senator said. "But I also thought, respectfully, that there was a disconnect between what he said today, particularly in regard to Iran, and things he has said and done earlier." Obama did not support the so-called Lieberman-Kyle amendment, which called on the U.S. administration to classify Iran's Revolutionary Guard as a terrorist organization.

Obama was angry with Lieberman, and at a meeting between the two expressed his disappointment at the tone and content of the assaults. He was a little worried at the time, early summer of 2008, because the polls were telling him that the Jews were less enthusiastic about him than they had been about previous party candidates. And such worries were especially evident in the Florida campaign.

But a summer-long battle ended decisively, when fall surveys put Jews right where they usually belong.[24] A Gallup poll revealed that nationally, the "proportion of U.S. Jews backing Obama is identical to the level of support the Democratic ticket of John Kerry and John Edwards received in the 2004 presidential election (74 percent)" and was "only slightly lower than what Al Gore and Joe Lieberman received in 2000 (80 percent)." More specifically, a Quinnipiac University poll of the Florida vote gave Obama a 77 percent to 20 percent lead over McCain in the Sunshine State.[25]

As for 2012, signs in Florida thus far are also not very encouraging for Republicans. The Jews didn't vote in the Republican primaries, proving that the constant talk of change in party identification is not yet evident in Florida to an extent that could have any electoral impact. Clearly, the Jews of Florida weren't moved by GOP candidates, they weren't moved by the party, and they weren't moved by Obama's policies — not enough to switch party registration and vote for their candidate of choice. Nevertheless, calculations of possible doomsday scenarios keep appearing in the papers. "If Obama receives only 68 percent of Florida's Jewish vote, which is what a recent Gallup poll showed him earning nationally, it could mean 20,000 fewer Florida votes than he received in 2008," warned The Tampa Bay Times in midsummer.[26]

So yes, one can imagine a Florida showdown in which every Jewish vote counts. But all in all, it is worth remembering that thus far no presidential election in U.S. history has been determined by Jewish voters flocking to one side or the other. Counting Jews, counting them in the crucial states, counting those that can be swayed to the other side, counting those that can make an electoral difference — counting all those hardly explains all the coverage and noise associated with the Jewish vote. But if counting isn't the way to measure the importance of the Jewish vote, what is?

* * *

Over the last several decades, Democratic Party identification overall has fluctuated, from 36 percent at the high points, in 1988 and 2008 (according to Gallup poll tracking), to a low of 31 percent in 2010.[27] Among many traditionally Democratic groups, such as white Southerners, Catholics and others, the trend has been fairly consistently downward, even as other groups, mainly Hispanics, have become more reliable supporters of the party. But while others were busy changing affiliation, the Jews' political leanings have remained largely the same. "Twenty percent of Jews line up with the Republican candidate, 60 percent with the Democratic candidate. About 20 percent are uncommitted to a particular party," explained one writer.[28] This is not exactly accurate today, but is close enough to make the point.

There are many explanations for the unique political behavior of the Jewish voter, most focusing on the relatively liberal views of Jews on almost all social issues, while others suggesting that the "rural, overwhelmingly Christian and Southern" nature of the GOP is a turnoff. The Washington Post's conservative columnist Jennifer Rubin framed it thus: "They don't sound like us, they don't talk like us, and they don't understand us."[29] Whatever the reason, the outcome is quite clear, and the number of Jewish votes at play seems small.

Will 2012 prove to be any different? In August 2011, New York Times op-ed columnist Charles Blow — relying on data from the Pew Research Center — argued[30] that "the number of Jews who identify as Republican or as independents who lean Republican has increased by more than half since the year [Barack Obama] was elected. At 33 percent, it now stands at the highest level since the data have been kept. In 2008, the ratio of Democratic Jews to Republican Jews was far more than three to one. Now it's less than two to one."

In response to criticism from some quarters, Blow repeated his claim a few weeks later in another column, in which he argued that "Obama's approval rating among Jews in 2010 averaged 58 percent. This percentage was the lowest of all those representing his enthusiastic supporter groups except one, the religious unaffiliated." Blow's claim that Obama's loss of support among Jews should be attributed to the president's positions on Israel was furiously debated. (Many of Blow's critics were associated with the dovish JStreet lobby, and relied on many polls in which Jews rank the topic of "Israel" as fairly low in their voting priorities.) Nevertheless, the question remains: Are Jews — as Pew researchers argue[31] — "the only ▢religious group analyzed in which the percentage who identify themselves as ▢Republican (as opposed to leaning toward the GOP) has risen significantly?"

To help make all this a numbers-based type of discussion, we pulled together and analyzed data available from four sources,[32] and the result was quite revealing: While Pew studies suggest that the GOP is gaining somewhat among Jewish voters (that was the basis for Blow's argument) and the other data is more nuanced, all polls end up pointing at similar numbers.[33] The Republicans, hoping to gain from Jews' disappointment with Obama's economic record or with Obama's positions on Israel, or to be the beneficiaries of Jewish demographic trends — the growing Orthodox population and the growing significance of the more conservative Russian-Jewish population — have about 27–29 percent share of the Jewish party identification. About 8 percent of the Jews sit on the fence, and the others identify with the Democratic Party.

Having said that, and knowing that party identification is the best projector of voting behavior, the picture is quite clear: On a good day, Mitt Romney has a glass ceiling of about 35 percent; on not as good a day, he will outperform McCain by 1 percent and get 27 percent of the Jewish vote. Pollster Jim Gerstein, simulating an Obama-Romney race in November of 2011, predicted an Obama lead of 63 percent to 24 percent.[34] And when Gerstein, a Democrat, allocated "the undecided voters by party identification — a common practice among political pollsters when trying to map out the outcome of a race," he split the vote so: 70 percent for Obama and 27 percent for Romney.

Other pollsters have had somewhat rosier predictions for Romney at other times. According to the AJC survey, Romney could get as much as 33 percent of the Jewish vote. But since we've already showed how small the number of undecided Jews is, it is clear that the number of voters that could still be transferred from one candidate to the other is miniscule. Just calculate: If the Jewish swing votes in play are no more than 8 percent,[35] Romney's ceiling is close to the mid-thirties. But for him to get to that number, one needs to give him the votes of every single undecided Jewish voter. And that's not quite realistic. If Romney gets half the votes of undecided Jews, he'll be around 30 percent. This means 4 percent more than McCain's 2008 vote, and, in places like Ohio, might mean a four-percentage-point increase within the 3 percent Jewish vote. A tiny fraction of voters. So — again — why even bother?

Yet interesting to note, the candidates bother. In this election cycle a lot of fuss has been generated about the highly publicized investment by Las Vegas casino magnate, philanthropist and billionaire Sheldon Adelson.[36] Adelson's dissatisfaction with Obama's policies, both domestic and foreign — especially those related to Israel — led him to pledge to unseat the president, even, he vowed, at a personal cost of as much as $100 million of his $24.9 billion fortune.[37] Adelson's pro-Israel credentials are sound, as partisan as they may be. He is close to Netanyahu and the owner of the pro-Netanyahu Hebrew-language daily, Israel Hayom (Israel Today), but also a long-term donor to more consensual causes, giving $25 million to Yad Vashem, and up to $140 million to Birthright.

The 79-year-old magnate first began to cause serious ripples when he popped up backing Newt Gingrich in the Republican battle to secure the party's nomination as presidential candidate. "I might give $10 million or $100 million to Gingrich," Adelson told Forbes at the time. He later declared that "no price is too high" to oust the Democratic incumbent. And it didn't end there. With Gingrich out of the running, Adelson soon transferred his loyalties to Romney, by then the clear winner of the race for the nomination. Adelson and his wife, Miriam, initially donated $10 million to the Super PAC backing

Romney. The money he decided to give for Jewish political outreach was a bonus.

His largess did not sit well with Democrats, traditionally the recipients of major Jewish donations. During the hot summer of electioneering, the National Jewish Democratic Council blasted Adelson over allegations that he had allowed prostitution at his casino resort in Macau, China. The fallout was swift: Adelson launched a $60 million lawsuit for defamation against the NJDC. Jewish organizations and avowed Obama supporters, Alan Dershowitz among them,[38] urged the organization to apologize, saying the accusations were "outrageous." And ultimately, apologize the Council did, although the whole incident left a new air of nastiness that is unusual in American Jewish politics.[39]

With Adelson's money, the Republican Jewish Coalition, headed by Matt Brooks, initiated an advertising campaign in some of the battle states in which Jews live in high proportions, such as Ohio, Pennsylvania and, of course, Florida. In this series of ads entitled "My Buyer's Remorse," Jewish Obama voters are shown switching sides because they are disappointed with the economy or with his other policies, notably relations with Israel. A $6.5 million campaign — and for what? To get the 4 percent of the 3 percent to switch sides?

Probably not. It is hard to imagine people as smart as this wasting money on a campaign of no likely consequence. There must be another reason — or reasons. And since the number of voters we're talking about is fairly small, the explanation must have to do with a small number of people making a big enough difference to matter.

* * *

Three such reasons are worthy of mention.

The first one — call it the "every-vote-counts" explanation — is the one relevant primarily to Florida votes in a very tight year. That Jews haven't yet tipped an election doesn't exclude the possibility that one day they might.

The second reason — the one that is mentioned by the experts more than all others — is Jewish money. Jews have high incomes compared to other American groups[40] and are a highly engaged group politically. This includes donating to political parties and causes. One 2011 study of the Jewish electorate found that "one in two respondents had given money to a political party."[41] And the givers, says veteran columnist Jim Besser, are of a very certain type: "While Jewish voting isn't very Israel-focused, Jewish campaign giving is — and especially the mega-giving that is playing a bigger role than ever in Election 2012."[42] In other words, if Besser is right, then the money Adelson is giving is really more an investment than a gift: he is giving his good Jewish money to the Republicans to bring on board more Jews who will give them even more money and, more importantly, not give to the Democrats, who heavily rely on it. According to some reports, "campaign donations from Jews or Jewish and pro-Israel groups account for as much as 60 percent of Democratic money."[43] That's reason enough for both parties to court the Jewish vote.

This was evident in a race as remote from presidential drama as is possible, and seemly quite insignificant as well: the House race of Arizona's 9th District, or, to be precise, the Democratic primary race of a newly created congressional district in the Phoenix suburbs. Two Jewish candidates were in the race along with Krysten Sinema, a onetime "radical left-wing activist who donned pink tutus at anti-war rallies and organized with anti-Israel groups,"[44] for which she got into some trouble. Observers of this race became concerned about Sinema and Israel. Not that she alone could tip the House against Israel, but, considering her record, they told me, she could make trouble. She could become one of the more vocal voices against Israel if she won the race. Her opponent, Andrei Cherny, argued that "Sinema's longtime associations with far-left-wing groups make her a dangerous woman to put in Congress." She has a "10-year track record," he said, "of taking positions that are at odds with American policy and administrations of both parties."[45]

The 36-year-old candidate — and the ultimate winner of the primary vote — denied all insinuations and allegations.[46] When embarrassing e-mail messages by her were revealed by the Jewish Journal[47] casting doubt on the sincerity of her Israel-related message, she fought back, writing of "a proven record of support for Israel" and promising a "strong ⬚voice for Israel in Congress." She fought for votes from local Jews who might consider her views on Israel unacceptable (Sinema, among other things, "helped create several groups that oppose the U.S.-Israel alliance"[48]), but no less was fighting against her opponent's attempts to get the attention of national media, and a national audience, for the race because such attention means one thing only — the ability of a candidate to raise funds in amounts regularly unavailable in local races.

In 2012, one could see how what Besser described as "Israel-focused Jewish campaign giving" was moving in the direction of Democratic races such as the one in Arizona 09, as well as in the direction of Republican candidates such as Senate contender Josh Mandel of Ohio, a highly competitive race and "among the most expensive" in the nation this year.[49] It is obvious that for final numbers from the 2012 campaigns, one will have to wait a little longer, until all races are concluded. But some numbers from past years are available for those interested in tracking Jewish funds. One example: Pro-Israel political contributions, including funds to Political Action Committees, or PACs, reached almost $14 million in 2008 and close to $13 million in the 2010 midterm cycle, about 35 percent of which goes into GOP-leaning organizations and 65 percent to Democratic organizations.[50]

Republicans, then, have a long way to go if the goal is to take money away from Democratic-leaning organizations. But one can't blame them for trying. In recent years they have become more efficient and have a higher profile, as they attempt to attract more funds from the "distinctive Jewish conservative voice emerging on Israel-related matters and an array of domestic social issues."[51]

* * *

Apart from the more tangible votes and money, though, a third factor seems to be in play as the significance of the Jewish vote is hyped time and again, and as the level of coverage of Jewish voters and analysis of Jewish calculations far outweigh its significance compared to other American sub-groups. Some would say it's the influence that Jews have in the media and their solid presence in notable positions. Others would point to their presence in celebrity circles and the arts, while still others would look to the over-representation of Jews in American politics as advisors, consultants, pollsters, analysts and elected officials.[52]

But really you can just go back to the example of the Iowa vote, and call it the bellwether factor. Jews are seen as major political players because they believe that their vote really counts, because they project self-importance. They might not tip elections, but they appear as if they can. "Focusing on presidential elections since 1980," wrote historian Jonathan Sarna,[53] "it appears that about 30 percent of Jewish voters may be characterized as swing voters, swayed by general as well as Jewish issues, particularly the economy, Israel, and church-state issues. When the majority of these voters swing toward the Republicans, it sends a warning to the Democratic Party."

Such a "warning" might come in many guises. In a post-2008 election conference call with Jewish Republicans — who had to face the undeniable truth that a vast majority of Jews, yet again, had voted for the Democratic candidate — the Republican Jewish Coalition leaders had an interesting case to make.[54] Because of our fierce campaign to sway Jewish voters, they said, the Democrats had to invest much more effort in the Jewish vote this time. Moreover, the concerns the Democrats had about Obama losing Jewish voters made the candidate more prone to give pro-Israel speeches. In essence, the Jewish Republicans were trying to take some of the credit for the making of the pro-Israel Obama. And that's not as preposterous as one's initial gut response might dictate. Politicians understand pressure: Obama was pressured, and he made the necessary adjustments; namely, he was more attentive to Jewish concerns — or at least more attentive to the need to reassure Jewish voters.

Obama could have easily won the 2008 election without the Jews, but losing Jewish voters would have projected badly on him, would have raised doubts, would have provoked unnecessary negative attention. Obama wanted to get the Jewish vote. All candidates want to outperform expectations with Jewish voters for the same reason that they all want to exceed expectations in Iowa. The Jewish vote is a symbol. For Democrats, who get the majority of it, it is a symbol of tradition and well-being. For Republicans, struggling to increase their share, a symbol of possible success with the general public.

In the 1988 race between Michael Dukakis and George H. W. Bush, the Republican candidate was running against a Democratic candidate who was never very popular with Jewish ⸮voters, and was the successor of a president who was (relatively speaking) ⸮popular among Jews. Reagan got more than 30 percent of the Jewish vote on two occasions; Bush, running on Reagan's coattails, crossed this threshold once. The second race, he lost the Jews — and lost the election.

That is not to say that where the Jews go America also goes. But it is interesting to note that there's a big difference in the number of winning GOP candidates who had ⸮30 percent of the Jewish vote and in losing GOP candidates who had 30 percent of the Jewish vote. Among the winning candidates were the 1988 Bush, the 1980 and 1984 Reagan, the 1972 Richard ⸮Nixon, the 1952 and 1956 Dwight Eisenhower. However, the last losing GOP candidate to get more than 30 percent of ⸮the Jewish vote was Charles Evans Hughes in 1916. So you see, there's good reason for Romney to invest in the

Jewish vote. If he gets 30 percent or more of the Jewish vote — not an easy benchmark — it is almost like getting an insurance policy against losing.

Or it could be the end of a very long political tradition.

2. Unlocking Jewish Sensitivities

March of 2008, and the fierce battle between senators Hillary Clinton and Barack Obama was leaving its mark on Jewish communities all over America, pitting old against young, more traditional against more liberal, those more worried about U.S.-Israel relations against those far more concerned with domestic issues. It was a sunny, breezy Sunday afternoon in the Beachwood suburb of Cleveland[55] when two panelists took the stage to represent the two Democratic candidates in a debate aimed at the Jewish community of the area. Some 150 people were in the room that day, most, so I assumed, aged 60 and over, and wearing a Hillary Clinton button, some even in Hebrew.

Congressman Adam Schiff of California represented the Obama camp; the now infamous former Congressman Anthony Weiner of New York spoke for Clinton. It was an entertaining debate — as entertaining as it was duplicitous, especially on issues related to Israel. Obama, bragged Schiff, speaks his mind, whoever the audience might be. He, Schiff, was representing a truth-teller. That may be so, but the same could not be said about Obama's surrogate — Schiff. Take, for example, a simple question Schiff was asked: Does Senator Obama oppose Jewish settlements in the occupied territories?

The answer that Schiff should have given was simply, "yes." Of course Obama opposes settlements, as we have all learned in the years since that long-forgotten little debate. But on the eve of a crucial Ohio primary vote, the Obama representative seemed to prefer caution to candor. Schiff did not say that Obama supported the settlements — he did not attempt an outright lie — he just refrained from applying his candidate's philosophy of truth-telling. Obama, he assured the crowd, had never criticized the settlements as being the obstacle to peace. Nor would he. Take Schiff's word for it.

Weiner was no better than Schiff (and yes, four years and a couple of raunchy sext messages later, that hardly sounds like a compliment to Schiff). When asked to explain Clinton's settlement policy, Weiner calmed the apprehensive Cleveland Jews with two promises: one, that Clinton would always respect the judgment of Israel and its citizens, and two, that she would move the American embassy to Jerusalem, something her husband, President Bill Clinton, did not do. It was hard to know if the people in the room really bought into this ridiculous pre-election spin, but I didn't see Weiner blush. Listening to Weiner that afternoon, I thought he sounded more like a representative of Republican candidate Rudy Giuliani than a Clinton emissary. And the more hawkish Weiner sounded, the more Schiff felt the need to follow his lead. Does Obama support the division of Jerusalem? No. And may I remind you, he will not dictate the terms of a peace deal. Call it cheating, or spinning, or just political professionalism, this is what

Jewish surrogates do on behalf of their candidates when elections are looming.

Israel and the related Middle East affairs were discussed in length at that event, but the crowd seemed more interested in hearing about domestic issues, on which the debaters only spoke toward the second half of the debate. This is a common feature of such Jewish political gatherings. The speakers mistakenly think that Israel is what the crowd wants to hear about, so they spend, or waste, the time discussing it instead of talking about the real issues that concern most voters.

Two weeks later in the campaign, as Obama and Clinton appeared at the American Israel Public Affairs Committee (AIPAC) annual conference in Washington, it was natural for the both of them to speak mostly about Israel and the U.S.-Israel alliance. But some differences were gradually emerging between the two. While Clinton was "following a tried-and-true rule of hers from New York — support Israel to the last," Obama was opting for "a more delicate strategy."[56] Earlier, in Iowa, the candidate had dared to speak about the "suffering" of Palestinians ("Nobody is suffering more than the Palestinian people"), for which he was immediately criticized by guardsman of the pro-Israel patrol. "Awarding first place in the suffering matrix is odious and infelicitous,"[57] Rabbi Steven Silver of Redondo Beach, California, told The New York Times. But such harsh criticism did not completely deter Obama from sticking to what he thought was the right approach. The candidate who was building his campaign around the audacity of hope couldn't just talk about dangers and troubles and enemies of Israel without giving some hope. "One of the enemies we have to fight," he said at the AIPAC conference,[58] "is not just terrorists, it's not just Hezbollah, it's not just Hamas — it's also cynicism."

Hearing both Clinton and Obama that morning, I predicted that "Obama will get more of the Jewish vote (if he doesn't stumble later on in the race)" and that "Clinton will get more of the Israel-related Jewish money." My reason for such a prediction back then still holds true today, as one ponders the 2012 election: Obama's message was more in line with the views of the liberal Jewish masses; Clinton's message was the right one for the established, older and more conservative Jewish donors. His message was the more attractive for the "naive, idealistic, tikkun-olam-now, Let's-fix-Darfur-first, we-need-to-engage-Iran, get-the-hell-out-of-Iraq mob — but this crowd is not the one giving money to candidates based on their position on Israel;" her message was "tailor-made for a smaller group, but one that's much more dedicated to Israel as a primary issue of concern."

My prediction was not accurate to the final detail, but it was close. Obama got more of the Jewish vote than most observers assumed he would. Later that same March, a Gallup analysis revealed that the two candidates had almost identical support among Jewish Democrats.[59] Later still, in May of 2008, Clinton was leading just slightly against Obama among Democratic Jews, not long before his ultimate victory.[60] She went on to handily win the Jewish vote in her backyard of New York and New Jersey (and Pennsylvania[61]); she also won in Florida and in Nevada. But Obama got close in Arizona and had a majority of Jews voting for him in the more liberal communities of Massachusetts, Connecticut[62] and California.[63]

When Obama ran in the general election against the Republican nominee, Senator John McCain, he had to overcome many of the allegations, insinuations and doubts first cast by the Clinton campaign. These were mostly related to Israel, and initially did seem to have had an impact on Jewish voters. In June of 2008, half a year before Election Day, Republicans were enthusiastically spreading the word: Obama's in trouble. Just 62 percent of Jewish voters had said at the time that they'd vote for Obama, much lower than the percentage of Jews voting for all preceding Democrats since Jimmy Carter in 1980.[64] Indeed, Jewish voters seemed to have been hesitant during the summer of 2008, before ultimately making the decision to support Obama in percentages as high as those of his Democratic predecessors.[65]

Why did all those hesitant Jewish voters eventually board the Obama train? That is a question worthy of some inquiry, as it is still very relevant. The summer of 2012 — just like that of 2008 — was heavy with Obama-in-trouble talk. A Gallup survey released in June[66] had revealed that "Obama appears to be doing worse among Jews than he did in the last election." His percentage in that poll: 64 percent — again, very much like the one he had in the summer of 2008, but about 10 percent lower than the 74 percent[67] of Jews who ended up voting for him in November.

Thus, if McCain had reason to believe in the summer of 2008 that more Jews would be voting for him than the business-as-usual percentage of Republican candidates, Mitt Romney also had reason to believe in the summer of 2012 that he would be the beneficiary of more Jewish voters. If McCain's belief back then was based mostly on his alleged superior friendliness toward Israel, Romney's belief in the summer of 2012 was also based on his alleged superior friendliness toward Israel. If McCain thought that Obama was vulnerable because of statements and associations that seemed questionable to many pro-Israel voters, Romney thought that Obama was vulnerable because of real actions that seemed questionable to many pro-Israel voters. But since McCain was ultimately disappointed by the vast majority of Jewish voters, the question for Romney remains: can he outdo his Republican predecessors and win over more Jews than McCain? Does he have the key with which to unlock Jewish voting patterns?

* * *

The 1868 election was "the first presidential campaign to focus widespread national attention on the Jewish vote," wrote the renowned American Jewish historian Jonathan Sarna.[68] Then as now, pundits greatly exaggerated the size and possible influence of that vote; then as now, they exaggerated the level of Jewish coherence and unity.

A number of prominent Jews supported the Republican candidate of the time, General Ulysses Grant — not an intuitive choice considering Grant's previous behavior toward Jews. As Sarna documented in "When General Grant Expelled the Jews,"[69] the general, concerned about constant smuggling between the North and South, decided to expel all Jews from the war zone. "In his correspondence, the word 'Jew' and the word 'smuggler' became almost synonymous," Sarna told me.[70]

To him, the parallels between 1868 and 2012 seemed almost obvious: "In 1868, Jews who had supported the Republican Party since Lincoln's first term faced a difficult conundrum. Should they vote for the Democrats, a party they considered bad for the country, just to avoid voting for a man (Grant) who had been bad to the Jews? The Democrats sought to roll back Reconstruction and disenfranchise Black voters. Should Jews vote for them anyway, just to avoid voting for a candidate who had expelled Jews from his war zone? The question of loyalties — how much should 'Jewish considerations' sway Jewish voters, and how much should they vote on the basis of what they see as good for the country as a whole — was hotly debated in 1868.

It seems to me that in the 2012 election, Jews will face some of these same kinds of questions."

Researchers Steven Cohen and Sam Abrams have asked Jews about their voting intentions and considerations, both in 2008 and regarding the 2012 election. And reading their studies, one can't escape the conclusion that the questions presented by Sarna hardly bother Jewish voters today. Jewish "considerations"? Cohen, Abrams and Veinstein[71] present an "alternative to issue-stances" as they focus their attention on a concept they term "political identity." That is, "how do Jews (and others) label themselves politically?"

In their account, Jews don't even have to think much about the issues — whether Jewish issues such as "tikkun olam" and "Israel," or general interest issues — as they go to the polls. "For non-Orthodox Jews," Cohen and Abrams wrote in their study of the 2008 Jewish vote, "Democratic Party affiliation and liberal political views derive from ethnic attachment and ethnic embeddedness." Put more simply, "the Jews' support for the Democratic candidate has less to do with their stances on the issues, and more to do with their historic, passionate, and highly significant commitment to the Democratic Party and the liberal camp in America." But even if issues are presented as the driving force, even then the level of "Jewish" concerns seems to be quite low among Jewish voters, as one can learn from Cohen and Abrams' 2012 study.[72]

American Jews today are pointedly more liberal than the overall population, the authors write, especially on economic issues traditionally considered to be social justice concerns. As their study goes on to examine Jewish voting intentions, the picture becomes even clearer: "As with other Americans, party affiliation matters: Democrats say they'll vote for Obama, Republicans for Romney, and Independents are split." Since there are more Jewish Democrats then Jewish Republicans — about three times more[73] — Obama has a clear advantage over Romney. However, party identification doesn't tell the whole story. Cohen and Abrams identified "three other dimensions, all related to progressive political attitudes" with which to foretell the vote of an American Jew: commitment to social justice, defined as "views on abortion, the environment, same-sex marriage, and health insurance"; commitment to economic justice, defined as "views on taxes being unfair, raising taxes on the affluent, the threat of banks, siding with labor unions, and the need for the government to help the poor"; and finally, "economic Conservatism," a term that stands for "concern for high taxes, the business climate, and jobs."

Naturally, those more strongly concerned about social justice would, broadly speaking, be "more inclined to support Obama over Romney." Jews today might not be as liberal as they were a decade ago, because of demographic changes, but they are still one of the most — if not the most — liberal constituency. If their priorities are domestic, if their concerns are social, if they are well within their political conform zone, then voting for the Democratic candidate is intuitive.

And 2012 priorities, indeed, are domestic: "The most important issue for Jewish registered voters ahead of the 2012 election is the economy," reported an April survey.[74] Fifty-one percent of Jewish respondents said that the economy would be their top priority in this election cycle, a priority quite similar to that of most Americans. (Jobs is often alluded to as the number one issue for most Americans.[75]) Another 15 percent of Jewish voters cited "the growing gap between the rich and the poor" as their top issue, and 10 percent mentioned health care and the deficit. All other issues garner far less attention: Israel, 4 percent; the danger of Iran, 2 percent; and the environment and immigration, 1 percent apiece. 2012 is an election about economy and jobs for most Americans, Jewish voters included. For Mitt Romney to find this hidden key with which to release the Jewish lock on Democrats would require much more than talking about his affinity for Israel.

In fact, it might just require far more than any Republican candidate can possibly give. The authors of the Solomon Project Report on Jewish American Voting since 1972[76] cite a "number of possible explanations for Jews' increased support for Democratic presidential candidates since 1992" — when Jews started voting overwhelmingly for Democratic candidates. (All candidates since Dukakis have received 74 percent or more.) However, they tend to believe that the most profound of those possible drivers of Jewish votes is the fact that since the early 90's, "the GOP became more strongly influenced by the religious right." In this report's telling, "in the 1992 election, evangelical Protestants solidified their Republican proclivities, becoming the core voting bloc in the GOP coalition," and even more important, "Republican candidates at all levels increasingly aligned themselves with the evangelical community, as well as with its social and religious agenda, one that the Jewish community perceives as inimical to its domestic interests." In other words, Republican candidates were presented with a nonstarter: take your chances with winning over a few Jewish voters, or align yourself with the most important Republican block of voters.

That candidates choose evangelicals over Jews is hardly surprising. That they keep up the effort to also increase their number of Jewish voters is somewhat intriguing.

* * *

In the Democratic debate of February of 2008, the moderator, the late Tim Russert, heated things up[77] by pressing Obama on the endorsement he had received from the anti-Semitic African-American leader Louis Farrakhan.[78] "On Sunday," Russert began, "the headline in your hometown paper, Chicago Tribune, declared that 'Louis Farrakhan Backs Obama for President at Nation of Islam Convention in Chicago.' Do you accept the support of Louis Farrakhan?"

"You know," Obama said, that "I have been very clear in my denunciation of Minister Farrakhan's anti-Semitic comments. I think that they are unacceptable and reprehensible. I did not solicit this support."

But "do you reject it?" Russert wanted to know. "Well, Tim," Obama responded to laughter from the crowd, "I can't say to somebody that he can't say that he thinks I'm a good guy."

You know that Farrakhan called Judaism a "gutter religion," insisted Russert.

Yes, Obama confirmed. "I am very familiar with his record, as are the American people. That's why I have consistently denounced it."

Enter Hillary Clinton.

If by the time of this debate anyone doubted Hillary Clinton's intention to use insinuations and past associations by way of scoring points against Obama in the Jewish community, this debate gave all the necessary proof. "You asked specifically if he [Obama] would reject it [the endorsement] and there's a difference between denouncing and rejecting," Clinton argued. Namely, Obama was merely denouncing Farrakhan instead of rejecting the endorsement. "I have no doubt that everything that Barack just said is absolutely sincere," Clinton icily remarked, "but I just think, we've got to be even stronger. We cannot let anyone in any way say these things because of the implications that they have, which can be so far reaching."

What was she trying to say — that Obama was somewhat anti-Semitic? Let's assume she was just thinking that Obama was playing politics and trying not to offend Farrakhan's supporters as he denounced his views. In any case, in this exchange Obama ultimately got the upper hand: "If the word 'reject' Senator Clinton feels is stronger than the word 'denounce,' then I'm happy to concede the point, and I would reject and denounce [Farrakhan]," Obama said. Cue applause.

This small incident paled in comparison to Obama's need to explain and overcome many later questions emanating from his long relationship with Reverend Jeremiah Wright. It merits re-examination only because of the smart nuanced message Obama was able to sneak into this seemingly problematic grilling over the Farrakhan endorsement. This was not the first time Obama had spoken about the issue of Jewish-black relations. He had rehearsed it a few days earlier, during an appearance before a group of Ohio Jewish activists. Talking about Farrakhan — and about anti-Semitism among African-Americans, which he had also denounced in an earlier speech on Martin Luther King Day — Obama touched a sensitive nerve when he discussed one possible consequence of his candidacy: the chance to restore the alliance between blacks and Jews. The "reason that I have such strong support" among Jews, Obama had said, "is because they know that not only would I not tolerate anti-Semitism in any form, but also because of the fact that what I want to do is rebuild what I consider to be a historic relationship between the African-American community and the Jewish community."

This is, I wrote after observing Obama speak at the time, "one promise that no American liberal Jew can simply ignore." Restoring black-Jewish relations has great significance, and the fractured relations are an open wound in the glorious story of Jewish American liberalism.[79] If Obama could heal such a wound, it would mean a lot to many Jews.

My interest, though, was ignited by the candidates' demonstrable understanding of Jewish American sensitivities. Yes, Obama also kept talking a lot to Jewish crowds about Israel, but he was shrewd enough to understand what his emissary in Cleveland, Adam Schiff, obviously didn't — or maybe Schiff was just hesitant to test the assumption that the Jewish vote isn't about Israel, that Jewish voters have more sensitive buttons that can be pressed. "You know," Obama said, "I would not be sitting here were it not for a whole host of Jewish Americans who supported the civil rights movement and helped to ensure that justice was served in the South. And that coalition has frayed over time around a whole host of issues, and part of my task in this process is making sure that those lines of communication and understanding are reopened."

Obama had the wisdom to give Jewish voters some pride that is unrelated to Israel, to give them some hope that is Jewish but also domestic, to remind them that they and Obama are both members of the same community of "justice."

And no, he probably didn't win the Jewish vote of 2008 because of this specific answer in that specific debate. But he did win smartly by neutralizing possible problems — be it Farrakhan or Israel — and turning them into advantages. Many Jews' ties to the civil rights era "apparently led them to value the historical significance of the Obama candidacy," concluded Prof. Steven Windmueller in a post-election analysis.[80] Jewish voters "used this opportunity to realign themselves with African-Americans and others in launching a new era in American political history." As election results made clear, "Jewish voters across the nation joined with African-American and Latino voters to shape a new Democratic Party coalition of minorities." And Windmueller believes that such a development "rekindled memories" of earlier eras, the "Roosevelt and Kennedy eras, when coalitional politics enabled the Democrats to win national elections."

* * *

At the end of the Cleveland debate with which I opened this chapter, Congressman Weiner, the Clinton surrogate, tried to pull the trigger on Obama's Israel policy. "We might not win the fight but we have to fight it," he said, because of the danger of having a candidate with such a compromised approach "when it comes to Israel." You know what kind of a president such a person would be? he asked the crowd. "A Jimmy Carter." We will get back to the Obama-Carter comparison, but first, some more needs to be said about the priorities of Jewish Americans.

3. What Jews Choose

When Oscar Solomon Straus was appointed by President Theodore Roosevelt to be Commerce and Labor secretary, a page-one story appeared in The New York Times with the headline, "Oscar S. Straus in Roosevelt Cabinet; Will be the First Jew to Hold Such a Post in This Country."[81] Born in Bavaria, Straus immigrated to the United States in 1854, first to Georgia and later to New York City.[82] He graduated from Columbia Law School and began his involvement in politics first at the local level, by supporting a mayoral candidate, and later by backing governor Grover Cleveland's presidential election.

Cleveland was the first to appoint Straus as minister to Turkey, a position he would later hold under two subsequent presidents. In 1906, Roosevelt named him secretary of Commerce and Labor, no doubt for his great skills, but also, as Roosevelt readily admitted, for his religion. As Straus later testified, the president told him that, "I have a very high estimate of your character, your judgment, and your ability and I want you for personal reasons. There is still further reason: I want to show Russia and some other states what we think of Jews in this country."[83]

Straus was "genuinely proud of his Jewish heritage," writes Naomi W. Cohen in her biography of him.[84] But heritage to him was not a confining straightjacket, as Straus "fused his Jewish ideals with his interpretation of Americanism." He "defined Judaism" as a source from which to draw ideals. In this, he anticipated a century in which political ideologies and Jewish religious ideals were combined, at times to the point of being barely recognizable as separate entities. "Religious and prophetic principles of social justice" were helping Jews in framing a "liberal political agenda."[85] For many Jews in America — Jews in other places, notably Israel, have other interpretations of Judaism[86] — the "values and ideas of liberalism resonated with the messianic principles of Judaism."

Prof. Jack Wertheimer of the Jewish Theological Seminary artfully mocked these tendencies and interpretation of Judaism, as he outlined the new "ten commandments" of America's Jews.[87] "It is no coincidence that the ideas and attitudes embodied in the new American Judaism are largely indistinguishable from the cluster of ideas and attitudes that inform liberal American culture at large," Wertheimer writes. His, of course, is a more conservative outlook. For others, there is no mockery involved in making political causes the manifestation of Jewish ideals. Ira Forman, formerly the head of the National Jewish Democratic Council, and in 2012 the Obama campaign's point man on Jewish affairs, once told me[88] that "within the Democratic Party individual Jewish Americans are active in a number of public policy agendas: health care reform, Darfur, separation of church and state, education policy, reproductive rights, civil rights, foreign policy, etc. The party's leadership does not see these agendas as particularly 'Jewish' issues. However, one of the reasons the party is engaged in an issue like Darfur is because there are so many Jewish political activists who are passionate about this issue."

Indeed, in the current election cycle, President Obama's health care reform comes to mind as one of the best examples with which to trace the Jewish unwavering support of Democratic administrations, legislators and agendas. Unpopular with much of the general American public, the battle over health care reform was one of Obama's most politically exigent legislative achievements. In the late summer of 2012, more Americans still held an "unfavorable" view of the "health reform" than a "favorable" view of it (47 percent to 42 percent in a Washington Post survey[89]). More Americans thought that they were "worse off under the health reform law" than those who believed they were "better off" under the law (30 percent to 26 percent). More Americans thought that the "country as a whole" would be "worse off" than those thinking the United States would be "better off" under the law (37 percent to 36 percent). The health care reform was one of the prime reasons for the trouncing of the Democratic Party in the midterm 2010 election.

While there was some debate concerning the exact level of support that the Democratic Party got from Jewish voters in the 2010 midterms, there was not much doubt that Jews overwhelmingly supported the party. And they supported health care as well. In Florida's heavily Jewish 19th District, where early elections were held in 2010, a

Republican candidate and an Independent candidate were both trying to convince the elderly Jews that health care reform was bad for them. We have "a high number of seniors in our district, and the current health care legislation, which I absolutely do not support, would clearly put our seniors in either financial difficulty or a lack of care," Jim McCormick, the Independent, told me.[90] It did not end up as he had hoped: The Democratic (and Jewish) candidate, Ted Deutch, won handily, proving that Jewish voters in the district were "as Democratic as ever."[91] The Solomon Project, later analyzing the FL-19 vote by precinct, focusing on those with the highest number of Jews, noted that, "despite the decline in support for the president among all voters nationwide over the course of the last year, Jewish voters in these precincts maintained their support for the Democratic congressional nominee of 2010."[92]

Jews did not abandon the Democratic Party in 2010 for two reasons. One, they listed the health care reform high on their list of priorities — 80 percent cited it as "very important" just before the election[93]. And they still do today: in a March 2012 poll by the American Jewish Committee,[94] 49 percent of American Jews listed health care or the economy as the most important issue that would decide how they voted in November (20 percent and 29 percent respectively). Two, most of these Jewish voters sided with the president and wanted to safeguard the reform. "Widely seen as the key domestic cause for American Jews," as one report defined it, health care reform has several national Jewish groups actively lobbying for it. "Among them is Jewish Federations of North America, the umbrella organization for the nation's local Jewish philanthropic federations, which are deeply involved in funding health care."[95] When one survey of both Jewish Democrats and Republicans asked respondents to say if they "support the president's efforts to create a national health care program," almost all Democrats, 1038 to 13, said yes, and, interestingly, a majority of Republicans, 442 to 270, also said yes.[96]

And they did it for religious reasons, or at least often used the language of religion as a way of explaining Jewish support for this political reform. Rabbi Julie Schonfeld of the Conservative Movement's Rabbinical Assembly went so far as to say that, "The president's vision is consistent with Jewish tradition, which is unambiguous about the requirement of a just and decent society to provide a basic level of health care." And such language did not end with the passage of the controversial legislation. When the Supreme Court largely upheld the president's health care reform, the move was met, again, with broad approbation by American Jewish organizations. While not always using the same language, many were stressing that universal health care was key in traditional Jewish values.

The national president of Hadassah, Marcie Natan, said that the organization "recognizes that lack of coverage compromises the health and economic well-being of millions of uninsured individuals, as well as our nation as a whole." Rabbi David Saperstein of the Religious Action

Center of Reform Judaism said, "We are elated that the Supreme Court has ruled in accordance with the laws of the land and past precedent to maintain the integrity of a health care system that provides better access to health care for so many Americans." The Jewish Council for Public Affairs stated that "universal, affordable and accessible health care coverage for all Americans remains a compelling policy goal and moral imperative."

To critics of the blurring lines separating Judaism from liberalism, this is yet more proof that Jewish organizations no longer represent the true interests of a Jewish community. In the United States, many leaders in the religious realm seem to have much more interest in political battles than in the advancement of traditional Jewish practices such as prayers and holy days. "Don't keep kosher, that's fine; don't keep Shabbat, that's fine; marry a non-Jew — whatever. But understand that it will take away your Jewish identity if you don't fight for justice," one Reform rabbi was quoted as saying.[97] Approvingly or disapprovingly? — the original tone doesn't matter much. It is for each individual Jew to decide.

* * *

In his masterly "The Making of the President, 1972," Theodore White chronicles, among many other stories, Hubert Humphrey's last presidential hurrah. "When he talked of his record," White wrote, "his sponsorship of civil rights, of Food for Peace, of nuclear disarmament, of student loans, of Medicare and Medicaid, of minimum wages, of Social Security, or rural electrification — one leaned forward, listening, half expecting Humphrey to tell how he had helped Ben Franklin invent electricity."[98]

Humphrey was friend of the many groups comprising the Democratic coalition of the 60's and early 70's; he was a friend of "the Masons and the Catholics; of the black and the Jews." White accompanied him when he spoke to "the aging Jews in the palm-fringed poorhouses of south Miami Beach during the Florida primary," reminding them that the credit taken by other candidates for the many good deeds of the party was all really his. "You know what I mean," White quotes Humphrey. "The children, they grow up and go away. Everyone says what fine children they are, everyone takes credit for them, the way they act, the way they talk. But they don't remember their parents anymore … people forget their parents in politics too."

The Jews ended up voting for the man who beat Humphrey to the nomination — George McGovern — in smaller numbers than the usual percentage a Democratic nominee gets from Jewish voters (but in much higher percentage than the rest of the electorate). In fact, McGovern ushered in the two decades in which the Jewish vote was more consistently conservative than in all other decades since the 20's. Surveys indicate that between 32 percent (CBS) and 37 percent (NBC) — 35 percent is commonly cited — of Jewish Americans voted for Richard Nixon in 1972.[99] When Jews believed that the Democratic candidate was too radical, and when this candidate didn't pass even the gentlest test of support for the Jewish state, the Jewish voters of the 70's made a decision that is quite remote from the current atmosphere in most Jewish circles. This is even more impressive considering the fact that Jewish party identification with the Democratic Party was at its peak in 1972 — 68 percent.[100]

Looking at the main issues on which the 2012 election will be determined, there's not much doubt as to where most Jews will be standing, compared to other Americans. At the end of August, more Americans said that Romney would "better handle" the economy.[101] Obama's economic job approval was definitely a weak spot — 53 percent disapproving, 39 percent approving.[102] But the Jewish picture (and one should note that there aren't enough polls of Jewish Americans from which to draw an accurate up-to-date picture) seemed quite different: almost an image in reverse. Of those Jews polled, 57 percent approved of the way Obama is handling the economy, while 42 percent disapproved.[103] On the question of which party the respondent felt would make the right decisions on the economy, 62 percent said Democratic, and 36 percent said Republican. (For the same question on health care, 66 percent said Democrat, and 32 percent said Republican.)

On the economy, Jews, as in the famous Milton Himmelfarb quip (whether it was really him saying it is another matter),[104] "earn like Episcopalians but vote like Puerto Ricans." Here's why: in the 2012 Workmen's Circle poll, when asked whether they would support an increase of the income tax for those making more than 200,000 dollars a year, 65 percent of Jewish respondents said that they were in favor of such a raise.[105] Prof. Kenneth Wald, writing about the consistency of the Jewish vote in the last 60 years, briefly referred to the Himmelfarb witticism, as he tried to explain why Jews are different on economics from other American groups. Going back to the 1948 Truman victory, Wald writes about the voting patterns of religious groups. "Catholics, Jews, and Baptists were Democratic by margins of two to one or better." The "five denominations that we would classify as mainline Protestants" were Republican "by equally lopsided ratios" at that time. African-Americans in 1948 were "evenly split in loyalty between the two parties."[106]

Sixty years later, Wald writes, "almost nothing is the same." Baptists are now strongly Republican, while "Catholics and African-Americans have traded places, the former now divided almost evenly between Democrats and Republicans and the latter overwhelmingly favoring Democratic candidates." Mainline Protestants are now more inclined to support the Democrats. "Every group had changed but one." Truman got 90 percent of the Jewish vote to Dewey's 10 percent. The 2008 Obama got a little less, but the vast majority of Jews still voted for him. The stability of

Jewish political loyalties, as Wald defines it, is no less than "stunning."

Like Wertheimer, though, Wald doesn't quite accept the idea of Jewish alignment with Democratic ideals because of "an affinity between core Jewish theological tenets — most notably tzedakah, Torah, and tikkun olam — and liberal political ideals." But while Wertheimer and others' criticism is more ideological, Wald's is factual.

The ideological objection to the theory opposes the interpretation of political agendas as if they were Jewish teachings. "And so it goes," another objectionist, Hillel Halkin, angrily wrote [107]: "Health care, labor unions, public-school education, feminism, abortion rights, gay marriage, globalization, U.S. foreign policy, Darfur: on everything Judaism has a position — and, wondrously, this position just happens to coincide with that of the American liberal Left."

If Halkin had read the 2012 poll of Jewish values by the Public Religion Research Institute,[108] it would probably would have made him even angrier. In this study, the authors just assume, without even bothering to justify their assumption, that the five notable Jewish values on which Jews should comment are pursuing justice, caring for the widow and orphan, tikkun olam, welcoming the stranger, and seeing every person as made in the image of God.[109] All these, of course, can be counted as Jewish values, but all are also values that are not markedly Jewish. Sixty-eight percent of respondents to this survey said that they would be attending Passover Seder this year — a sizable majority, but not as sizable as those saying that pursing justice is an important value (84 percent) that informs "their political beliefs and activity," and not as high as the number of Jews saying that tikkun olam (healing the world) is an important value (72 percent).[110]

Tikkun olam has long become synonymous with Judaism in America. It was picked up by many Jews including some who are hardly involved in religious practice. The mayor of New York City, Michael Bloomberg, "cited his commitment to tikkun olam as one of the reasons for his plan to reduce air pollution in Manhattan by charging special fees for vehicles entering congested parts of the borough."[111] And Obama is constantly utilizing it, associating himself with it. "It's refreshing how genuinely and naturally our president relates to the Jewish community," wrote one of the cofounders of Rabbis for Obama. "He mentions by name responsibilities like tikkun olam, the Jewish tradition of working to repair the world, and then talks from the heart about his belief in the same. He discusses the concept of 'hineini' — 'Here I am' — not only because he thinks giving an unexpected d'var Torah makes for a good speech, but because he subscribes to the values those prophetic words represent."[112]

Whether Halkin is right to be outraged at what he perceives as the hijacking of Judaism for the promotion of political agendas or not, Wald's interpretation of the "weakness" in the Jewish-value-based theory of Jewish political behavior — his objection to it — is different. "If Jewish liberalism is the product of Jewish historical experience/values/minority consciousness," Wald writes, "it should be the major motif of Jewish politics elsewhere. Yet only American Jews show this consistent political preference for the left while Jews in other democracies sometimes divide equally between left and right, mimic the rest of the electorate, or favor the right." Thus, his explanation of the consistent Jewish alliance with the Democratic Party takes him elsewhere, and focuses on Jews' interest in maintaining the regime of separation between church and state (more about this issue in the next chapter). Still others have other explanations.

Yet the bottom line is always the same: When it comes to most domestic issues of debate, Jews are one of, if not the, most liberal groups in America. Eighty-nine percent of Jews, for example, believe that abortion should be legal in all or most cases (45 percent and 44 percent respectively[113]) — compared to 53 percent of the general American population, to 39 percent of Republicans and to 65 percent of Democrats.[114] In other words, Jews support abortion rights much more strongly than the average Democratic voter.

And they also support gay marriage more than the general public: While support for gay marriage is on the rise generally, the camps of opponents and supporters of those "willing to allow gays and lesbians to marry legally" are almost equal: 47 percent support, 43 percent oppose, with 22 percent strongly holding a position in each of the camps.[115] Again, Jews are not just supportive, but much more supportive of a legal change: 81 percent of American Jews "support allowing same sex couples to marry legally, including more than half (51 percent) who say they strongly favor same sex marriage."[116] No wonder that most Jewish organizations responded favorably to the president's endorsement of gay marriage.[117] The National Council of Jewish Women, Hadassah, the National Jewish Democratic Council, the Reform Religious Action Center and the United Synagogue of Conservative Judaism all praised the president for his publicly stated new position. "President Obama has admirably continued to demonstrate the values of tikkun olam in his work to make America a better place for all Americans," NJDC Chair Marc Stanley said, as he demonstrated, yet again, what tikkun olam has come to symbolize.

* * *

In June of 2012, both Obama and Romney were in Ohio to outline their economic plans for the coming four years. The choice of venues was as telling as the content of the two speeches: Obama went to a community college, Romney spoke at a small business. Obama said that "the debate in this election is about how we grow faster, and how we create more jobs, and how we pay down our debt. That's the question facing the American voter. And in this election, you have two very different visions to choose from."[118]

That has been Obama's strategy of recent months: to convince the voters that two markedly different worldviews are competing in this election — his and Romney's. Romney, Obama says, has "disdain" for green energy,[119] an issue of great importance to many Jewish voters (only 29 percent of them oppose environmental protection even in cases where "it raises prices or cost jobs"[120]). Romney, Obama says, has "extreme positions." Romney, he says, "is proposing a $5 trillion tax cut that disproportionately goes to the wealthiest Americans."

Romney, meanwhile, initially attempted to make the election about one person: Obama — and about his record of failure and his flawed policies (according to Romney). But Obama kept forcing Romney into a two-way contest. For Obama, it was important to make sure that voters don't just decide if he is a success or a failure, don't just examine his record and make a decision based upon that. He realized, assisted by public opinion polls, that this record is not convincing enough for many voters. Thus Obama kept hammering on his message of choice, painting Romney as some kind of an economic extremist: "Yes, there have been fierce arguments throughout our history between both parties about the exact size and role of government — some honest disagreements. But in the decades after World War II, there was a general consensus that the market couldn't solve all of our problems on its own." Romney,

Obama was saying, is offering you a solution that is beyond the pale of this consensus. Romney will be ripping the American social fabric instead of sewing it back together as needed.

Of course, Romney came to this election not as an ideologue but as a manager, the CEO who will put the house back in order without much consideration for party politics. The record he is highlighting is all about business experience and running Massachusetts and saving the Winter Olympics. Romney is trying to be the solid executive America calls to unburden it of a president who has failed to fix the economy. That he had to shift rightward during the primary season so as not to be beaten by the candidates more solidly and more explicitly conservative makes such a position a little more difficult to maintain. That he decided to pick Paul Ryan, an outspoken proponent of economic measures that most Jews will be hard-pressed to even consider supporting, and an opponent of all abortion, makes him less attractive to those who might be willing to consider a moderate managerial type.

"Romney's best hope for reversing the GOP's declining Jewish fortunes would have been to remind American Jews of the cultural and economic moderation he showed as Massachusetts governor," wrote Prof. Peter Beinart[121] (not a Romney supporter, I presume). Moreover, "were he still the Romney of a decade ago — pro-choice, pro-gun control, pro-gay rights, and pro-universal health coverage — he might be on his way to grabbing 40 percent of the Jewish vote." Alas, presented with the choice between the Jewish vote, attractive as it might be, and the core beliefs of the majority of Republican primary voters, Romney didn't have much of an option. He has a party to consider.

And this party will be the topic of our next chapter.

4. Romney's Party Problem

Todd and Jamie Ehrenreich were interviewed not long after John McCain lost them "in one fell swoop."[122] Both were registered Democrats but were going to vote for the Republican candidate, for fear of losing money if Democrat Barack Obama were elected. All this changed, though, when McCain picked as his running mate a women who "doesn't know what she's talking about and makes it up as she goes along," as Jamie defined it. And she was hardly alone in this opinion. The nomination of former governor of Alaska Sarah Palin for vice president sparked a barrage of such quotes and the subsequent anecdotes of McCain losing the Jewish vote. Jews, concluded columnist Jennifer Rubin two years after the fact, just "hate" Palin.[123] "It is not an exaggeration to say," she wrote, "that, more so than any other major political figure in recent memory (with the possible exception of Patrick J. Buchanan), she rubs Jews the wrong way."

Two days before the 2008 election, I went to see a Palin rally at the McKinley high school in Canton, Ohio. Country singer Gretchen Wilson was there, performing "Redneck Woman" in front of a cheering crowd of three hundred or so Ohioans. It was, of course, a cheering crowd of losers — deep down they all knew that they were about to see Obama get elected. But they also knew "Redneck Woman" by heart and sang along to pass the time until the vice presidential candidate showed up.

"Palin's status as an unabashed conservative and as exemplar of the religious right would have been sufficient to alienate the majority of American Jews," Rubin would later write, "yet if that were all, and that is plenty, Palin still would not provoke the degree of hostility with which most Jews regard her." American Jews, she observed, "are largely urban, clustered in Blue States, culturally sophisticated." In other words, much too sophisticated to be supporting a redneck-by-choice candidate.

Palin is Romney's problem with Jewish voters. Not her specifically, but the shadow she casts over the Republican Party, the shadow cast by her supporters and followers, by Tea Party activists and conservative talk-show hosts, by staunch evangelicals, and their pastors and organizations. The party is Mitt Romney's problem with Jewish voters —. the Republican Party in which religious Christians have a greater voice, in which heartland America has a greater voice, in which Palin can be a candidate, in which Paul Ryan can be a candidate, and in which conservative Rick Santorum can be a serious contender in the primaries.

In late 2006, not long before the midterms, I traveled to Butler, Pennsylvania to meet with Santorum.[124] A few visitors were wandering around the sun-drenched Butler square that day, among its several memorials. Paying their respects to the fallen of war after war, from the American Revolution to Iraq, whose list of names was still growing, etched in wood instead of stone. And looking at another memorial, with a car engraved at the top — the car that is the pride of Butler, where the first Jeeps were manufactured. When I was there, though, it was for another transportation-related event — the groundbreaking of a new bus terminal, attended by town elders and the guest of honor, Senator Santorum.

Later that evening, a conservative television commentator called Santorum "the Winston Churchill of our times." So I joined this present day Churchill, on a surprisingly warm afternoon, as he wore an open collar, gave a short speech and turned over a shovelful of dirt. On that day, Santorum seemed to know that the battle for his seat was probably over. He was helplessly swept away in the wave washing over his party. And no, it didn't happen to him because of his extra bit of conservatism alone. Not too far west, a moderate Republican from Ohio, Mike DeWine, also lost his seat.

Santorum has been one of Israel's most important friends in the Senate. And that's what he was trying to use as his trump card with Pennsylvanian Jewish voters, clustered around Philly and Pittsburgh. It did help him some with getting large donations (by some estimates Santorum got more than $2 million) from pro-Israel donors,[125] but according to the Pennsylvania exit polls, only one out of five Jews actually voted for Santorum in the election he lost to Democratic candidate Bob Casey, Jr. The friend-of-Israel argument fell short, the same way it failed in most recent election contests in which

Republicans were attempting to use it against Democratic opponents.

Republicans can reliably claim that Republican voters give the U.S.-Israel alliance more support and attention than their Democratic counterparts. A recent Pew survey measured the extent to which Americans want the United States to support Israel.[126] Respondents were asked to indicate if this support should be more than it is today, less than today, or about the same — and the outcome was telling: "a plurality of the public (46 percent)" said that the support is about right; 22 percent said "the U.S. is too supportive" and a comparable percentage (20 percent) said "it is not supportive enough." But significant differences between Republicans and Democrats were evident. Almost 40 percent of Republicans did not believe that the United States is supportive enough of Israel (38 percent, to be precise), but only 8 percent of Democrats and only 4 percent of "liberal Democrats" shared this view. In another poll, about a year earlier,[127] 58 percent of Republicans said they consider Israel an "ally," compared to just 29 percent of Democrats. More Democrats defined Israel as "friendly but not an ally" (40 percent, compared to 26 percent of Republicans), but almost 20 percent of Democrats defined it as "unfriendly" (8 percent) or even an "enemy" (9 percent).

Hence, the common interpretation of Romney's July 2012 visit to Jerusalem as an attempt to specifically win over Jewish voters barely holds water. Romney came to

Israel for many reasons, but the ☐most important reason is as simple as this: He needed to go someplace, and Israel is as good a place as any.[128] ☐In the summer before elections, presidential candidates often go to foreign countries so that voters will get a taste of them as the potential ☐leader of the free world. They need to be seen boarding airplanes, landing in places to which most Americans have never traveled, meeting foreign leaders — preferably leaders with whom American audiences are somewhat familiar. And even better, foreign leaders whom more Americans like than dislike. Like this guy from Jerusalem — Benjamin Netanyahu. In a Gallup poll published before the Romney trip, 35 percent of respondents viewed Netanyahu in a ☐positive light, and 23 percent gave him a negative report card.[129] The only group of voters ☐who don't much like Netanyahu is the group in which Romney will not find many voters — Democrats.

Israel is a good place to visit for other reasons: The country itself is popular with the voters, especially Republican voters, as we've seen. The ☐candidate is not taking the risk of being associated with countries that most Americans do not like. And Israel is also relatively safe and comfortable, even while having an image of an embattled country under constant siege. This means that for Romney coming to Israel was ☐both quite easy but still carried some of the benefits a candidate would have from ☐visiting a combat zone. Unlike his visit (which he botched for no apparent reason) to London ahead of the Olympics — which everyone knows is more about pleasure than delving into serious ⬚diplomatic matters — in Israel one can talk about the issues that matter in foreign affairs: Iran, Arab Spring, terrorism, American power.

Thus, like Obama in 2008, then a presidential hopeful, Romney timed his pilgrimage to Jerusalem for the immediate run-up to the November election. Two men were behind the trip, as Allison Hoffman of The Tablet reported in detail[130]: Netanyahu's senior adviser Ron Dermer, a staunch Republican in his pre-aliyah days in Miami, and Romney adviser Dan Senor. The well-connected Senor had made a name for himself as a conservative politico, beginning with a stint as defender of George W. Bush's Iraq War, and as the co-author of "Start-Up Nation," a book detailing Israel's disproportionate technological successes. Hoffman chronicles how the Romney visit was cooked up by Senor and Dermer during a visit by the former to Israel in June.

Senor was close behind Romney and Israel's Washington Ambassador Michael Oren, when the candidate was greeted by Prime Minister Netanyahu in Jerusalem. Also in the entourage was Sheldon Adelson, whose deep pockets have given weight to his declared ambition to unseat Obama. Adelson switched his allegiance to Romney from party rival Newt Gingrich (whose ultimately fruitless presidential campaign survived for so long in part thanks to Adelson's largess), and was in attendance at the Romney's $25,000-per-head fundraiser in Jerusalem.

In Israel, Romney got the effusive welcome that befits an American presidential candidate. He met with Netanyahu — an old friend from their young consulting days in the 70's[131] — and was a dinner guest at the prime minister's home. His keynote speech, delivered as the setting sun turned the walls of the Old City golden behind him, was attended by some 150 carefully picked guests. The number included "religious American immigrants" and "Jewish American millionaires, settler leaders like the former chairman of the Yesha Council of settlements Israel Harel, and former Netanyahu aides."[132]

While the trip to Israel came after visits to staunch United States allies Britain and Poland, it was clearly the headline stop on the Romney foreign tour. Obama's Jewish support has been notoriously battered over the past three and a half years, and Romney's visit was perceived by many to be a play to woo Jewish voters. However, much of what has been written about the trip verges on hyperbole. First, Netanyahu did not endorse Romney when the two faced the media together, as some writers have suggested. Yes, he was a gracious host, but would anyone expect him to not be a gracious host to an American presidential candidate? Yes, Netanyahu made remarks implicitly critical of the Obama administration, but he was merely repeating his well-known positions.[133]

⍰

Nor was Romney guilty of making a huge gaffe, as many claimed, when he pointed to the "dramatically stark difference in economic vitality" between Israel and the territory under Palestinian Authority rule. "Culture makes all the difference," Romney said. "And as I come here and I look out over this city and consider the accomplishments of the people of this nation, I recognize the power of at least culture and a few other things." It was impolite for him to say such a thing, for sure, and it could complicate his ability to reach the Palestinian public should he win in November, as could a video leaked September 19 in which Romney tells attendees at a May 2012 fundraiser that the Palestinians are not interested in peace. But such statements are hardly a faux pas among Romney's circle of supporters. In Republican eyes, they only help make the claim of Republican Israel-friendliness — a claim that, as we've seen, hardly works with Jewish voters to begin with and that Democratic candidates have found an easy way of neutralizing altogether.

There is a simple "me too" tactic that many Democrats have been using in recent years to take Israel off the table as a voting consideration for Jews. Some still claim that Republican policies really hurt Israel — that a more interventionist approach is what Israel really needs — but many others stick to a much simpler message: not to claim that Republicans are no friends of Israel but rather to offer praise of their stalwart support for the state, proclaim similar tendencies and suggest to move to other topics, on which there is real difference between the parties.

Just before the 2010 midterms, I traveled to Illinois to write about multiple races, among them the one between Democrat Dan Seals and Republican Bob Dold.[134] It was a very close race; Seals eventually lost, but the district is competitive again in 2012, as Dold struggles[135] to defend it against Democratic candidate Brad Schneider.[136] Heavily Jewish and suburbanite, the district only became available to contenders when it was vacated by representative-turned-senator Mark Kirk.

I had a conversation with Seals on a Friday afternoon that started with an inevitable question about the discovery of a package of explosives that was sent to a Chicago synagogue the day before.[137] And Seals was, as expected, "disturbed by the possibility," the proper beginning for a conversation focused mostly on U.S.-Israel relations and Seals's view of Obama policy since early 2009.

The Democratic Seals had criticized the Democratic administration over the strained relations with Israel during a debate with rival Dold ("with a D not an E", as his campaign ad reminded voters who might think it was Bob Dole running in their district). But having detailed how he thought the Obama administration could do better, Seals also expressed the belief that Obama's "intent was good but [that] the strategy failed." His voters, he said, see Israel "as a local issue," especially

Jewish voters, despite the fact that not all of them support the exact same policy. "It is not a monolithic community and there are many point of views" — an issue we will discuss more broadly in the next chapter.

As for his rival, Seals had no problem in saying that Dold was also a strong supporter of Israel, as well as expressing the desire for Israel to "remain a bipartisan issue." This is evidence of that neutralizing tactic I've mentioned. It worked for Bob Casey against Santorum in Pennsylvania, and for John Kerry against George W. Bush in the 2004 election; now Seals was using it to neutralize Dold's pro-Israel tactic. "I know why some Republicans would like people to think that the Republican Party is better on Israel [than the Democratic Party] — but I don't believe this [to be true]," Seals told me. He said that most Jews do not buy such Republican propaganda. The proof is in the pudding: "If most of them still support the president and vote for the Democratic Party," it means that they think the support Israel is getting from Democrats "is fine."

* * *

In the eyes of many Jewish voters, the kind of support that Israel is getting from Republicans is not always a good thing, especially not so if one considers the reason for which the Republican field is so faithfully — an apt term — pro-Israel.

In mid-March, Christians United for Israel (CUFI) announced that it had passed the one-million-supporters mark.[138] I covered the launch of CUFI a few years ago, so I witnessed it growing until it became, by far, the largest pro-Israel organization in the United States. Like it or hate it (as many do), ignoring it is no longer an option. Not for Israel's government (this was never really in doubt — Israel will take whatever support it can get), not for other pro-Israel lobbies[139] (as Nathan Guttman so aptly put it,[140] "the shofar-blowing, hora-dancing Christian evangelicals are now an integral part of the pro-Israel advocacy scene"), and not for Congressional legislators. One million members mean that many representatives have a lot of CUFI members in their districts, ready to take action. CUFI has members in all 50 states and holds dozens of events every month in every corner of the United States. In Washington, its annual conference attracts more than 5,000 participants. It is powerful and is growing stronger.[141]

Thus, as one ponders the "growing Israel gap"[142] between Republicans and Democrats (in March 2012, 78 percent of Republicans sympathized with Israel compared to 53 percent of Democrats[143]), one knows that a lot of it is due to growing evangelical support for Israel, due to the work of the likes of Pastor John Hagee, CUFI's leader. That many Jews in America don't feel comfortable with evangelical support for Israel is not exactly new. Some of them do not like CUFI's embrace because of theological fears, others because of political differences. When CUFI was established in 2006,

Hagee's second in command, David Brog, explained to me in a long exchange[144] why Christian evangelicals support Israel, but readily acknowledged that "it is very hard for Jews to believe that Christians have suddenly embraced philo-Semitism in an honest and sincere way."

In terms of pure politics, this could be an even greater challenge. Most Jews in America, including many staunch pro-Israel Jews, support the Democratic Party and support Obama. And the Hagee troops (and Hagee himself) don't always make it easy for these Obama voters to see them as an ally. In the 2011 CUFI Washington gathering, the pastor insisted that "President Obama is not pro-Israel." When I asked Hagee more recently if evangelicals are more supportive than American Jews of Netanyahu, his response was diplomatic, but also revealing[145]: "He sure seems to get a warm ⬚reception from American Jews every time he speaks in America. But yes, it's certainly true that Christian Zionists admire Prime Minister Netanyahu a great deal. We have a lot in common. Like him we believe strongly in Israel's right to exist and right to self-defense and don't apologize for it. ⬚Like him, we believe that Israel must always bargain from a position of strength. And lately, we have one more thing in common: since he's been studying the Bible with his son, Prime Minister Netanyahu has been quoting scripture even more than a lot of clergy I know!"

To Hagee and many fellow evangelicals, the Mormon Romney began his presidential race as suspect — only

40 percent of all evangelicals consider Mormons to be Christians[146] — and might still be held as such. Thus, those searching for motivations behind Romney's Israel trip need not bother looking to Jewish voters. There are a lot more evangelicals than there are Jews in America, and evangelical support for a Republican candidate is a box that must be ticked. If Romney can't quite win over this vast pool of voters by the force of his religious beliefs, as Santorum and other candidates had a better chance of doing, he can still convince them that, on matters important to them, he will pursue policies they will find more palatable.

This game of pandering to evangelicals, a game of political necessity for Romney, is a killer when Jewish voters are considered. "For decades", as journalist Carl Schrag explains in his report on American Jews and evangelical Christians from 2005, "most American Jews have been vocal supporters of liberal positions on many domestic U.S. issues. American Jews have backed abortion rights, gun control, civil rights, gay rights, strict separation of church and state, and so on. They have also built many alliances with other like-minded groups to further these causes. Few of those alliances were built with evangelical Christians, because they have been on the other side of each of these issues."[147]

American-Israel writer Zev Chafets, who penned an entertaining account of his encounters with evangelical Zionists,[148] once argued in an interview[149] we did together that "the real reasons American Jews fear conservative evangelicals are political and social, not theological. Jews are a major stakeholder (perhaps *the* major stakeholder) in the Democratic Party; evangelicals are a major stakeholder (perhaps *the* major stakeholder) in the Republican Party. And many Jews still see evangelicals as dumb southern rednecks. There is a fair amount of snobbery and even (dare I say it) bigotry, in this stereotype," Chafets said. But he was right: Jews, as a recent poll demonstrated, do not have a very positive view of evangelicals. In fact, "they hold considerably unfavorable feelings toward members of the Christian right."[150]

As noted briefly in a previous chapter, the consistent and very wide gaps in Jewish voting patterns between Republicans and Democrats really began to emerge in parallel to the surge of the religious right as the major force in GOP politics. Prior to 1992, a majority of Jews voted for Democratic presidential candidates, but this was not a majority that was as clear and defined as from 1992 to 2008. In 1988, more than 30 percent of Jews voted for GOP candidate George H. W. Bush, and many of them abandoned him in the 1992 cycle. While most interpretations focused on Bush's rocky relations with Yitzhak Shamir's government in Israel as the core cause of this loss of support, it is interesting to note that 1988 was also the year in which evangelical political power started putting its real mark on Republican politics.[151] That year, "not only did the party's front runners actively compete for Christian right support, the movement also produced a candidate of its own, televangelist Marion G. ('Pat') Robertson."

When in the early 90's, "evangelical Protestants solidified their Republican proclivities, becoming the core voting bloc in the GOP coalition,"[152] Jews were less inclined to even consider the party as an option. On most domestic issues, the gap between liberal Jews and conservative Protestants was hard to bridge; Israel was neutralized as a voting issue; and cultural differences were making themselves markedly present in every report from every Republican political gathering. The fact that 2012 is less about social issues, such as abortion or gay rights, and more about the economy doesn't necessarily change things much. Not even on economic issues can Jews and evangelicals easily agree: while both Jews and evangelicals agree in about the same percentages that the government "should do more to reduce the gap between the rich and poor,"[153] 80 percent of evangelicals believe that "poor people have become too dependent on government assistance programs," compared to just 54 percent of Jews. The two groups, it should be noted, were the highest and lowest ranking on this issue in this survey.

And this metaphorical Republican cross now rests on Romney's shoulders as he attempts to gain Jewish votes.

* * *

In mid-September of 2011, special elections were held in New York's ninth district, due to an urgent need to replace disgraced Congressman Anthony Weiner. The Jewish congressman was forced out after he had been caught sending a "sexually suggestive"[154] explicit photo to a young woman, and two candidates emerged as the major contenders in this historically Democratic, and very Jewish, district. New York-09 has the fourth-largest Jewish population of any congressional district, according to a 2009 report. These voters, the representatives of a Jewish population of more than 173,000,[155] made up 25.5 percent of the vote.

Republican Bob Turner and (Orthodox Jewish) Democrat David Weprin fought bitterly for the seat, and as the race became tighter, Democrats of national prestige started parachuting in, hoping to make a change. They realized that the race was being closely scrutinized as a measure of public attitudes toward Obama. The Democratic Congressional Campaign Committee was pouring money in ($500,000 on television ads), and the Democratic group House Majority PAC spent an additional $100,000.[156]

As usual, the Jewish vote got the special attention it deserves and then some. Representative Henry Waxman of California, watching the race from afar, said the Jewish vote was a concern for his party. "There are Jews who are trending toward the Republican Party, some of it because of their misunderstanding of Obama's policies in the Middle East, and some of it, quite frankly, for economic reasons. They feel they want to protect their wealth, which is why a lot of well-off voters vote for Republicans."[157] In the New York-09 race, Democrats were left staring at their fears of Jewish abandonment coming to life.

Indeed, the race ended badly for Democrats, catapulting Turner into the House, and igniting the usual barrages of glee and doom from the respective political camps. A statement from Matt Brooks of the Republican Jewish Coalition explained that "this Republican win in an overwhelmingly Democrat district is a significant indicator of the problem that President Obama has in the Jewish community." Democratic Congressman Elliot Engel predicted following this race that the president would "still get a majority of Jewish votes, but I would not be surprised to see that drop 10 to 20 points."[158]

Such predictions have a long history of being proven wrong when the final tally is counted. And Republicans have a long history of building false expectations, based on various signs and indicators, only to be later disappointed.[159]

Prior to the 2004 Bush-Kerry presidential contest, some GOP strategists were led to believe that the president was destined to outperform many of his Republican predecessors and win more than 30 percent of the Jewish vote. They too had signs: In December 2001, a survey by the RJC was interpreted so positively for Bush, that it concluded that, "if the election were held today …

more Jews would vote for Bush — 42 percent — than for former presidential candidate Al Gore, who received 39 percent support." Of course, Gore did not run in 2004, and Bush lost in the Jewish vote to Kerry by margins similar to those of the Obama-McCain 2008 contest — another race in which premature signs gave the Republicans false hope. When 2008 spring and early summer polls indicated that McCain might have a chance of getting more Jewish votes than Bush, the wave of "Jewish problem" stories could not be stopped. But the votes never materialized, neither for Bush nor for McCain. Alas, in 2004 and 2008 Republicans had mostly encouraging polls to rely on, while the 2012 Republicans thought they had more: the actual vote in New York 9th.

However, what the NY-09 race truly meant, and still means, is a matter of some debate.[160] Many blamed the already vilified Weiner for the loss. Others thought this was a no-confidence vote related to Israel, citing a poll according to which 54 percent of district voters found the administration's policy on Israel to be disagreeable. Others had a different poll, which showed that very few voters in the district — 7 percent in all — considered "the candidate's position on Israel" to be "the single most important factor in choosing which candidate to support."[161] About half of Turner's voters listed the economy as their number one issue — an issue that is not important to Jews alone. "The voters' mood on the direction of the country, coupled with the unfavorable rating of President Obama — particularly among

Republicans and independents — makes this a tougher election for Weprin, or for any Democrat running in this district or a district like it," pollster Steven Cohen said at the time.

Whether NY-09 can be a bellwether on which to base another round of Republican expectations for a Jewish surge is questionable. Sure, the district has many Jews living in it, but the percentage of Orthodox Jews and immigrants from the former Soviet Union among them is high. These groups tend to be more conservative than most other Jews to begin with, and might not be the proper community in which to measure Obama's standing among Jewish voters. Obama himself carried the district in 2008 with a relatively mediocre 55 percent — barely better than the 53 percent he received nationwide, as Nate Silver noted.[162] With other Jews more instinctively liberal, the president might well fare much better in November than he did with the Jews of NY-09.

And besides, one can't compare the local race and pulling a lever for a Turner, to the national race and voting for a Romney-Ryan ticket.

* * *

It is time to talk about the Ryan factor.

When Paul Ryan was first presented to the public as Mitt Romney's choice for a running mate, there was a curious reaction: cheers on both sides of the political map. Republicans praised the bold decision to bring in someone who would not shy away from debating the real issues and presenting a real alternative; the pick of a candidate with a "Reagan-like quality," as columnist Charles Krauthammer described Ryan.[163] But Democrats, curiously, were also cheerful: They see in Ryan a manifestation of the scary Republican. He may be the nicest person on Earth, as many acquaintances testify, but he will take away your health care and your Medicare and your social security — with that youthful grin on his face all the while.

"To envisage what Republicans would do if they win in November," Ryan Lizza of The New Yorker wrote in his masterful profile of the VP candidate,[164] "the person to understand is not necessarily Romney, who has been a policy cipher all his public life. The person to understand is Paul Ryan." That's the message Democrats have been also been hammering home to Florida voters since Ryan was nominated. He is the man; he is the real face behind the Romney bureaucratic masque. Just as Sarah Palin stripped away McCain's cloak of moderation, forcing Jews back into the Democratic fold — as the argument goes — Ryan is stripping away Romney's cloak of moderation and pragmatism, and is giving Jews a real incentive to return to their old habit of voting Democrat.

Is it an incentive, or is it maybe an excuse?

As we saw at the beginning of this chapter, the story of the 2008 Palin negative effect on Jewish voters keeps popping up whenever there's reason for a diagnostic analysis of the inherent incompatibility of Jewish voters and Republican politics.[165] "As it turned out," explained a Daily Kos report,[166] "a key factor in John McCain's failure to get American Jews to choose him was his choice of Sarah Palin as his running mate." The Daily Beast chose to explain the story of the 2008 Jewish vote thusly[167]: "Obama has appeared to lag among Jews. ... But the Palin pick 'probably blunted any gains the Republicans had made.'"[168]

In short, Obama was in trouble, as documented by AJC surveys, but then McCain picked Palin, and the tide turned back to the left. That sounds reasonable: If one reads the 2008 AJC survey of Jewish opinion,[169] one might be tempted to believe this line of argument. In September, only 57 percent of Jews said that they'd vote for Obama, but something changed their minds between then and Election Day. Could it not be Palin? Is she not the most likely instigator of such change?

The answer, surprisingly, could be no. While it was natural for Jewish Democrats to say at the time that they "believe the nomination of Alaska Governor Sarah Palin has driven many undecided Jews back into the arms of the Democrats," the evidence isn't necessarily supportive of such a theory. But to understand why, you'll have to bear with me through the following piece of technical analysis. There certainly were Jewish voters who decided to go with Obama because of the Palin nomination, but most Jewish voters had jumped on the Obama bandwagon way before she was announced. And if one wants to truly understand this, all one has to do is abandon the AJC survey, which was both late and considered to be relatively conservative. The numbers released by Gallup tell a different story.

The Palin surprise came in late August of 2008, but, by looking at Gallup polls, one can clearly see that Jewish voters were abandoning McCain two months before that.[170] In July of 2008, McCain could read the Gallup polls and still hope for a 34 percent Jewish vote. In August, before the Palin pick, his numbers among Jews went down to 25 percent. That's pretty much the percentage of Jews who eventually voted for him. Palin neither added anything to nor detracted anything from the McCain pool of Jewish votes. The Palin effect then might be a Palin myth. That she was not well-liked in many Jewish circles is a given. But in those Jewish circles, very few were ever serious about voting for McCain, with or without the controversial vice presidential pick. It was more of an excuse, or a way of rationalizing one's vote, than the real reason.

And Ryan could do a similar disservice to Romney. Elderly Jewish voters in Florida are at the top of the list of those considered receptive to the Democratic message of Ryan's supposed dangerous radicalism. Hence, the instinctive response of many commentators, hurriedly tagging the Ryan pick as the reason for Romney's ultimate loss of the chance to win a larger share of the Jewish vote. "What Romney needed to do in his selection of vice president to unite his party is exactly the opposite of what he needed to do to make inroads among Jews," explained Raphael J. Sonenshein,[171] executive director of the Edmund G. "Pat" Brown Institute of Public Affairs at California State University, Los Angeles.

What's the problem with Ryan? That he just doesn't have "Jewish values," as three past presidents of the National Council of Jewish Women, Jewish Women International and the founding chair of the Hadassah Foundation complained.[172] As Jews, these interpreters of Jewish theology explained, "we feel obligated to live up to the principle of 'tikkun olam,'" and Ryan's policy proposals "conflict with our tradition's commitment to worldly justice." Nadine Epstein, editor of Moment Magazine, similarly explained that "for 5,000 years" the Jewish have practiced the kind of "community centered values [that] are at the heart of the liberal vision of society."[173] And while Jewish Journal's David Suissa aptly suggested not to ignore "other Jewish values, like living within our means and confronting difficult truths,"[174] but you'd be hard pressed to find many supporters of such a suggestion.

The circle is now complete then: it is not just conservative ideas related to church-state relations, or to morality, or to family life that are being presented as anathema to Judaic standards — apparently, economic conservatism is also against Jewish tradition. In other words, one cannot be a proper Jew and support a Rick Santorum-style morality; one cannot be a proper Jew and support a John Hagee philosophy; one cannot be a proper Jew and support a Paul Ryan economy; one cannot be a proper Jew and support the Republican Party.

That is, not the Republican Party that is Romney's 2012 party. This is Romney's Jewish problem.

5. Obama's Israel Problem

The 2012 Barack Obama is hardly the 2008 Barack Obama, but old themes die hard, and the case perpetuated against him in the Jewish community is not an unfamiliar one, with one caveat: if the 2008 warnings referred to what Obama might do, the case today is based on more evidence — what the president did, what he said, what damage he has already caused, what damage he could still cause. And like the ghost of presidents past, when speaking with Jewish Republicans about Obama, the same comparison keeps popping up: Carter, as in, Jimmy Carter.

Carter ranks as mediocre or worse in most surveys by U.S. historians of past presidents' "greatness," and ranks even lower in similar surveys of the public.[175] But among the American Jewish community, his name is more loaded. Carter got a fair share of the Jewish vote when he first ran for president in 1976 (64 percent), but his second run was the lowest point for Jewish Democrats in many years — 44 percent of the Jewish vote. (His rival, Ronald Reagan, got 37 percent.[176])

In fact, Carter didn't do very well with Jewish voters even in his first run. In eight of the ten presidential cycles between 1972 (Nixon-McGovern) and 2008 (Obama-McCain) "the Democratic presidential nominee ran between 22 and 32 points better among Jewish American voters than he did among all American voters." There were two exceptions to this rule: "the two cycles in which Jimmy Carter was the Democratic nominee."[177] Carter, the argument goes, was "an openly evangelical candidate of the kind that has put off Jews."

But Carter's first run aside, the big story of the Jews-Carter breach is the one from his second run. He was "the only Democratic candidate in 80 years not to win a Jewish majority (14 percent of Jews that year voted for third-party candidate John Anderson)"[178]. Truly, his troubles started even earlier, not with the contest against the charismatic Reagan, but rather in the fierce primary battle between Carter and Senator Edward (Teddy) Kennedy. This was a nearly successful attempt from within the party to unseat the president, in which Jewish voters played a significant role.

Polls taken in New York a month before the New York Democratic primary that year indicated that Carter would beat Kennedy in the state by a margin of 54 percent to 28 percent.[179] But this didn't exactly happen: Kennedy shocked Carter by winning New York (and Connecticut).[180] The Jewish vote had tilted heavily against Carter. In the summer of 1980,[181] when the battle was over, Howard Kleinberg of The Miami News began a report about Carter's Jewish problem with a quote from a Sylvia Hershkowitz, "a delegate to the national Democratic convention from the Bronx." Hershkowitz told him that "no Jew could ever vote for Jimmy Carter" and wondered about the Jews of Florida who had "voted for that man."

Kennedy beat Carter in New York by 59 percent to 41 percent. The Jewish vote was four to one for Kennedy. In Miami it was better for Carter — only two to one for Kennedy. In Connecticut, 56 percent of Jews had voted for Kennedy. Jews, like many Americans, were disappointed with Carter for many reasons, chief among them the slow economy. But they also had more focused anger, directed at his policies on Israel. American Jews were troubled by Carter's constant criticism of Israel, that has become even more vocal since, and by his contentious relations with then-Israeli Prime Minister Menachem Begin.

On March 1, 1980, as the primary contest was heating up, Carter's ambassador to the United Nations, Donald McHenry, "voted for a viciously anti-Israel resolution in the U.N. Security Council condemning Israeli settlement activity in Jerusalem,"[182] and Carter later "linked his loss in New York with his ambassador's support for the anti-Israel resolution at the U.N." His former aide and longtime supporter Kenneth Stein, breaking from Carter only in 2005, revealed what the former president told him about his long mistrust of American Jews[183]: "[Vice President Walter] Fritz Mondale was much more deeply immersed in the Jewish organization leadership than I was. That was an alien world to me. They [American Jews] didn't support me during the presidential campaign [that] had been predicated greatly upon Jewish money ... Almost all of them were supportive of Scoop Jackson — Scoop Jackson was their spokesman ... their hero. So I was looked upon as an alien challenger to their own candidate ... So I didn't feel obligated to them ... Fritz ... was committed to Israel ... It was an act just like breathing to him — it wasn't like breathing to me. So I was willing to break the shell more than he was."

In his "White House Diary,"[184] Carter reveals both anger and penitence over his rocky relations with Democratic Jewish voters. Carter testifies that he was "disgusted with the American Jewish community" for attempting to convince him not to sell arms to Saudi Arabia, and in retrospect believes that he would have "been better off if I had ignored" Jewish voters in 1980. But he also says, "I still have deep regrets about the fact that I alienated many American Jews during my time as president." This pattern of veering from denunciation to remorse and back did not end with Carter's departure from office. In books and articles he has written since, Carter has claimed that Israel was an "apartheid state,"[185] only to later ask for forgiveness[186] for "stigmatizing" the country.

That is one reason why the Obama-Carter comparisons, widely spread in punditry circles, resonate even more within the Jewish community (for those finding it valid). When the Obama-Carter comparison is made in general public settings, it evokes economic struggle, inefficacy and an "uninspiring president who is captive to, rather than captain of, events,"[187] as Jon Meacham, a Pulitzer Prize-winning biographer of presidents, defined it. For Jews, a "Carter" also revives the shadow of suspicion that Obama is a member of the "new Left" with its familiar themes of identification with the third world and with Palestinian narratives. And a "Carter" also evokes an ongoing uneasy relationship with the Israeli government, a troublesome Middle East policy, and — most relevant in the 2012 cycle — the ghost of Iran. Carter's undoing was greatly assisted by the Iranian hostage crisis and the disaster of Operation Eagle Claw, the failed and humiliating attempt to free the American hostages.

Obama is today facing a much different Iranian crisis — in many ways far more serious, in other ways one that has less impact on the coming election, at least as long as war does not erupt and American soldiers are not put in harm's way (more about Iran in the next chapter). The

Jewish community today is also not exactly the community of the 70's; many sectors within the community are far more critical of Israeli policy and seem far more willing to accept a president who is also publicly critical of specific governments and actions.[188] Many of these voters feel it's time to redefine what it means to be an American Zionist or an American Jew who supports Israel,[189] but does not feel obligated to unconditionally back Israeli policy.

In fact, Obama was one of the first candidates for such high office to have noticed and internalized this change within the Jewish community. In a quote made famous by concerned critics, the 2008 Obama explained to a Jewish gathering that, "I think there is a strain within the pro-Israel community that says unless you adopt a unwavering pro-Likud approach to Israel that you're anti-Israel, and that can't be the measure of our friendship with Israel."[190] Essentially, what Obama was saying back then — and his actions later were demonstrably in line with this sentiment — is that he does not agree with the policies of the Likud Party, and that he also doesn't think it is mandatory for someone to accept the policies of the Likud Party to be considered a friend of Israel. Obama as president — that's the version his supporters would endorse — has been both a critic and a friend.

And of course, candidate Obama was right when he said this: supporting Likud Party policies and supporting Israel are not the same. However, the fact that Obama mentioned a party by name, singling it out as an example, seemed problematic at the time and seems prophetic today. Obama was basically telling both American and future Israeli voters this: If Israel elects Benjamin Netanyahu prime minister and Americans elect Obama president, expect trouble.

Was Obama worried about the barrage of criticism within the Jewish community both during his primary battle against Hillary Clinton and later in his election campaign against John McCain? At times he seemed insistent on speaking truth to Jewish voters, as he was relying on this known change of Jewish priorities and sentiments and expecting Jewish voters to ignore insinuations and understand that he saw eye to eye with most of them on the majority of issues. After all, most Jews support the "two-state solution" and most Jews oppose Israeli settlement policies. At other times, though, Obama seemed shaken by the volume of criticism aimed at his Israel-related policies and statements. He seemed truly apprehensive of being Carterized by Jewish critics.

* * *

At the end of January of 2008, I was among a group of reporters invited to a conference call with then-candidate Obama.[191] Apparently, he felt an urgent need to talk about a "constant virulent campaign" that was being waged against him as he was fighting to win the party's nomination. This campaign, he told us, was aimed specifically at weakening support for him within the Jewish community. It included calling him a Muslim and accusing him of not pledging allegiance to the United States. And this campaign might be "getting some traction," he said.

This campaign haunted Obama all the way to the White House, at times clad in more civil clothes and focused on actual policies and true statements, at times becoming a more shady whisper campaign aimed at frightening elderly Jewish voters in Florida away from voting for him. And "Israel" had a lot to do with this constant barrage of criticism.

One example: Not long before Obama's conference call, one of his biggest Jewish supporters, Lee Rosenberg, was sent on Obama's behalf to Danny Ayalon, a former Israeli ambassador to the United States. He wanted to understand why Ayalon had written an article slamming the presidential hopeful — an article that raised hell in Israeli diplomatic circles.

Earlier in January, an Israeli newspaper (Maariv) had already run a lead headline claiming that Israeli officials did not want Obama to get elected,[192] that they didn't think he would be good for Israel. The sources were anonymous, and the content not very convincing. But later in the month, one senior former Israeli official decided to go on record with his doubts. Ayalon, just recently released from his ambassadorial duties, wrote in the Jerusalem Post that, "we should look at the

Obama candidacy with some degree of concern."[193] He also shared with the readers some details from his meetings with Obama, after which Ayalon "was left with the impression that he [Obama] was not entirely forthright with his thinking."

Rosenberg, a member of the AIPAC board of governors and an Obama supporter, did not quite like Ayalon's article, and did not quite understand Ayalon's claim that he had been misquoted. (Ayalon told him, though, that he maintained that Obama's inexperience in foreign affairs was a problem.) Rosenberg urged the former ambassador to become more familiar with the candidate and his history, and said he'd be happy to send him information. Ayalon, deputy foreign minister in the Obama presidency years, did not seem to need such information to be forwarded to him. For those as suspicious about Obama as he already was in 2008, Obama's actions as president were all the proof one needs.

Rosenberg was not the sole Obama emissary voluntarily caught in an exchange of Obama-Jewish fire. In mid-March 2008, former U.S. ambassador to Israel Daniel Kurtzer climbed onto the speeding Obama bandwagon, becoming a supporter and advisor.[194] With his new book "Negotiating Arab-Israeli Peace" just out in stores, the former envoy was the perfect decoder of Obama's future intentions toward Israel's region. However, Kurtzer was a statesman accustomed to serious discussion of problems in the Middle East, not to being a street fighter in political altercations. And this was evident when I saw him representing Obama before a Jewish audience at an assembly of the United Jewish Communities (today's JFNA).

While the Middle East and Israel were up for discussion at this event, the former envoy was diverted by the audience to the more pressing issue of the day: the extreme language that Reverend Jeremiah Wright had used. When it was revealed that Wright had spoken against America as well as against Israel, the "Wright crisis" was no longer a burden on the relations between Obama and the Jewish community. The whole of America was reflecting on the ties between the candidate and his spiritual leader. And Kurtzer was stuck in the middle.

He reminded the audience that Obama had already spoken, already announced that he did not agree with Wright. He also mentioned that this was not the first affair, nor the first slur against Obama. There are "nagging doubts, there are e-mails, there are innuendos: These are the kinds of things which we [Jewish Americans] as a community have suffered over the years at the hands of anti-Semites," Kurtzer had said, attempting to communicate to the Jews in the room that Obama was a victim in the Wright affair, not the aggressor.

This theme of victimhood — in many cases justified, in some not quite — would repeat itself many times during the 2008 campaign. In her much-celebrated "Great Schlep," comedian Sarah Silverman humorously ragged older Jewish voters for being hesitant about Obama for supposedly racist reasons.[195] Your "grandparents don't like Barack Obama," she said, "because his name sounds scary, sounds Muslim." In other words, it is not something Obama had said or had done that had made him a source of suspicion to older Jewish voters: it was all things beyond the candidate's control — his name, the color of his skin. (Silverman explained how her white "nana" liked the same things adored by young blacks.) And since his election, Obama has not been shy about playing the victim card in regards to his Israel-related policies. The argument would go like this: "Hawkish American Jews and hawkish Israelis misrepresent my views and actions. They are perpetrating a smear campaign to prove that I am not a true supporter of Israel, when in fact I am."

In the summer of 2009, rumors were spreading that the president would soon be traveling to Israel to better communicate his intentions.[196] The idea for this presidential trip (that never materialized) was based on wrong analysis: that Israelis just don't understand Obama, that they are suspicious of him because of false assumptions and too much exposure to misguided insinuations. But this was not exactly true. Israelis did not suffer from lack of understanding of Obama and the issues; they suffered from peace-fatigue, and they looked at Obama's policies with wariness that was based on experience and events. What Obama needed, if he wanted to calm Israelis, was a convincing plan that would make sense to them. And he didn't have one.

In March of 2009, soon after he became president, "Barack Obama told reporters that the efforts to bring peace 'will not be easier' with a government headed by [Benjamin] Netanyahu, but [that it] will not 'be less necessary.'" Indeed, no discussion of the Obama 2012 Jewish campaign can be complete without some measure of rehashing Obama's wobbly relations with Israel's government. Is he truly a friend of Israel? Can he be trusted to keep being such friend for the next four years? As we've previously argued, most Jews don't put Israel on top of their agenda as they go to the polls. But as was evident in the Carter example, Jews might still decide to forgo other issues when they feel that a candidate has not passed an unspoken litmus test of pro-Israeliness. Thus, at the heart of the 2012 Obama-Romney Jewish contest lies this debate: Is Obama Israel's best ally? Is he just reasonably friendly, or has the president been guilty of "throwing Israel under the bus"? [197]

* * *

After a very rocky start, a long and bitter slog, and an ultimate failure, the Obama administration slightly calmed its relations with the Netanyahu government. And this happened only when it became clear to the administration that the time was not ripe for a continuous fight.[198] Be it for political reasons (election, and the pressure from pro-Israel big shots), or reality on the ground (Arab Spring and other pressing matters), or just a change in priorities (one doesn't do Middle East peace when joblessness is at 8 percent), the second half of Obama's term was calmer than the first half. Below-surface tensions, though, were never eased. Obama and Netanyahu have a dislike for one another that is undeniable and evident to all.

In early 2009, senior members of the Obama administration did not celebrate Netanyahu's electoral victory. When the prime minister sent direct and indirect messages to the administration of his intent to "get along with" the new president, he received a chilly response. Obama had surrounded himself with advisers who were suspicious of Netanyahu, and didn't have much inclination to trust his good intentions. Many were veterans of the Bill Clinton administration — officials still trapped in the former president's peace narrative of the 90's. And in this narrative, Netanyahu had been cast as the villain who thwarted the peace process that was supported by the noble leader, the late Yitzhak Rabin; he was cast as a disruptive radical, as a man opposing peace and intent on keeping the occupation in place, as an unreasonable negotiator.

Obama had many advisers at the start of his term but little good advice: Former Senator George Mitchell was chosen as special envoy for Middle East peace based on his experience as chronicler of the first days of the second Palestinian intifada. The dowry Mitchell had in his briefcase was the document he had penned eight years earlier, and to whose conclusions — that there had to be a settlement freeze — he stuck all through his unsuccessful term as special envoy; Chief of Staff Rahm Emanuel, who is unlikely to have had many Israeli friends who voted for the Likud Party, was also a scarred warrior from the Clinton-era wars with Netanyahu; and, of course, Secretary of State Hillary Clinton, who during her husband's two terms did not show much affection for Netanyahu, but then mainly had praise for him during her stint as a senator for New York, with its fair whack of Jewish voters, many of them hawks.

In and among all this, Obama was planning a robust round of diplomacy. He thought he would pressure Israel to freeze settlement construction, take advantage of his popularity to coax gestures out of the Arabs, bring both sides back to fast-track negotiations and recruit the international community for assistance. He assumed — believed — that he could bring peace. And fast. Those who supported him believed it too, or pretended to believe it. The then-Egyptian President Hosni Mubarak said in June of 2008 that a "historic settlement is within reach" thanks to Obama's involvement in the peace process. And truly, the objective was attainable but for the fact that the American president forgot to take into account the two main protagonists: the Jews and the Arabs.

Obama and Netanyahu met for the first time in March of 2007. Obama was still a candidate; Netanyahu had not yet been elected to his second stint as Israel's prime minister. It was a short meeting, dictated by tight schedules, in a side room at the airport in Washington. Obama had just landed and Netanyahu was about to take off. It was a good meeting, primarily because of the well-chosen central topic of Iran. Obama was already a fervent supporter of tighter sanctions on Iran, and of course it was not hard for him to convince Netanyahu of this need. The Palestinian issue was not given more than a passing reference. Obama was a candidate in the ascendant, and there was no need for him to spoil the moment with troublesome matters.

Two years later, the first official meeting between Obama and Netanyahu, in May of 2009, was not as rosy. Most meetings since have also been frosty. The encounters, beginning with the first one, "exposed differences of opinion." As reporters informed their readers: "Obama expressed support for the principle of two states for two peoples, and Netanyahu declined to commit at this point." Obama told Netanyahu that "settlements have to be stopped in order for us to move forward."[199] Netanyahu didn't understand why Obama is so eager to deal with such a secondary issue when Iran keeps its centrifuges running.

Later, much later, there was some debate over the proper terminology suitable to describe the ensuing, for want of a better word, crisis ("there was no crisis," Israel's Washington ambassador, Michael Oren, said). What's clear is that the Obama team did not have many qualms about having an open quarrel with the Netanyahu government. In one preparatory conversation for the Obama-Netanyahu meeting, Emanuel reportedly advised Obama that he should not be scared "to trample on [Netanyahu's] head" a little, and according to another version of events, he might have even said that Obama should "break a bone," presumably one of Netanyahu's. In Washington there were many who believed that the president's ultimate aim was to pressure the Israeli government until it crumbled, and there was apparently someone in Jerusalem who believed it too — Netanyahu.

It was during these first months of contentious relations and constant pressure on Israel to freeze settlement activities that cracks began to appear in this hypothetically well-planned Obama strategy for peace, spreading doubt among some Obama officials as to whether the strategy was really working.

One such fissure followed the interview given by Palestinian President Mahmoud Abbas to Jackson Diehl of the Washington Post.[200] Diehl wrote: "Abbas and his team fully expect that Netanyahu will never agree to the full settlement freeze ... So they plan to sit back and watch while U.S. pressure slowly squeezes the Israeli prime minister from office." The Palestinians, some Americans had started to realize, believed rumors that were being fed to them from Washington. They heard the whispers and forgot that they were dealing with politics. They heard Hillary Clinton tell Al Jazeera that "we want to see a stop to settlement construction, additions, natural growth — any kind of settlement activity"[201] — and forgot that there's the other side to be considered, not just the American side.

That other side — Israel — was puzzled and angry with Obama. Puzzled, because it didn't understand what the Americans were trying to do. Angry, because the Obama administration, while pushing Israel toward a "freeze" also decided to ignore previous understandings between the Bush administration and the government of Ariel Sharon concerning the so-called "settlement blocs." Senior members of the Israeli government, and not just the hawks, responded with dismay to this move by the Obama team. This, they said, is not a matter of policy differences; it is a matter of trust. If this administration doesn't have any qualms about botching previous understandings, how can we trust it to honor future understandings?

There is an argument among Israeli officials that has not been settled to this day, and maybe won't be for many years to come: What exactly did Obama hope to achieve by sparking a row with Israel? The hardliners speculate that the president wanted to erect a barrier between Israel and himself in order to curry favor with the Arab world. The more lenient claim that it was simply an error in judgment. Obama, an adherent of the latter group says, listened to people who spoke "from the gut and not from the head"; that is, advisers who know little yet act decisively.

In June of 2009, Obama began in earnest his efforts to reach out to the Arab world, with an event that came to be known as the "Cairo speech."[202] Later the same month, Netanyahu responded with his "Bar-Ilan" speech[203] at the university of the same name. In the Israeli and American capitals, the respective speeches were discussed and dissected in an attempt to glean their true meaning. In Israel, there was a sourness because Obama's speech said that Israel's statehood was the outcome of pogroms and the Holocaust, not any historical or Biblical right. Thus, Netanyahu's speech included a rebuttal to Obama's argument: "The right of the Jewish People to a state in the Land of Israel does not arise from the series of disasters that befell the Jewish People over 2,000 years … The right to establish our sovereign state here, in the Land of Israel, arises from one simple fact: Eretz Israel is the birthplace of the Jewish People." (Obama, it should be noted, later corrected his own record in his speech at the United Nations, saying that "these facts can't be denied: The Jewish people have forged a successful state in their historic homeland."[204])

In Washington they weren't exactly jumping up and down either, following Netanyahu's speech. It took the prime minister too many months to say something even resembling support for the "two-state solution," and even then it was begrudging. Netanyahu got a message from Washington: without a "two states" statement, there would be no public appearance with Obama. "If the president will be standing next to Netanyahu without the latter publicly committing himself to the two-state solution, it will seem as if the president is willing to accommodate Israeli rejectionism," a senior official told me at the time.[205] Following Netanyahu's speech, it was only natural for some Obama officials to whisper in the ear of the president: "You see, only pressure works with this guy."

But a blow, not quite noticed at the time, had already marked the beginning of the end of the Obama initiative. In fact, it came the day before the all-important Cairo speech, but was drowned out by the noise surrounding the main event. On June 3, a day before Cairo, President Obama visited Riyadh, where he asked the Saudi king what gestures his government was willing to make in return for an Israeli settlement freeze. None, said the king, and then subjected Obama to a long, furious speech, whose severity even led his aides to later apologize to the American delegation.[206]

Awareness had begun to seep in, at least in some quarters. Even those who believed that Israel was being futilely stubborn on the settlements could not blame it alone: the Arabs had hardly demonstrated any greater desire to move ahead. They were sitting on their hands, waiting for Obama to make his move.

This didn't stop Washington from keeping up the pressure until, in August, Netanyahu agreed to a nine-month freeze on construction in the West Bank, not including construction in East Jerusalem. The Obama administration, for a short time, was hopeful again. There was one potential sticking point — the Palestinians' refusal to join negotiations until the freeze was a full one, that is, including East Jerusalem, but the Americans were still optimistic. At a meeting between special envoy Mitchell and an old Washington acquaintance the conversation went like this:

Acquaintance: What about [Palestinian President Mahmoud] Abbas?
Mitchell: That's my last concern.
Acquaintance: But won't he be difficult about speaking to Netanyahu without a full freeze?
Mitchell: He won't have a choice. He'll come.

* * *

This book isn't about the Israeli-Palestinian peace process or about Obama's failed attempt to advance the peace process. Therefore we'll take a shortcut to where we are today: the Palestinians did have a choice, and chose not to come. Israel would not agree to freeze settlement construction further once the nine months had expired. The American initiative ended in failure. By September of 2009, the Americans no longer had many expectations. They had managed to drag Abbas to a three-way meeting with Obama and Netanyahu, but they hadn't managed to change his stance.[207] He was angry at Obama for promising (as Abbas saw it) but not delivering.

And he was not alone in his anger. Trust between Obama and Netanyahu also never recovered. More misunderstandings and more bitter lecturing and more disputes kept popping up along the way — the Joe Biden visit that ended badly[208] and the 1967 lines speech that surprised and enraged Israel[209] are just two notable examples. More recently, the ongoing debate over Iran policy is in the limelight. But the freeze was both the high point and the low point in Obama's relations with the current Israeli government. He succeeded in curbing Israel's will but accomplished little, except for the lingering image of difficult relations that he is now trying to shake off.

He also achieved very little, politically speaking. In mid-2009, it was becoming clearer that Obama's treatment of Israel was having an impact on the more conservative American Jewish voters, including more conservative Democrats. In the annual survey of Jewish opinion conducted by the American Jewish Committee,[210] just 54 percent approved of the "Obama administration's handling of US-Israel relations." More American Jews — 59 percent — gave Netanyahu the seal of approval on handling the relations. Moreover, a major blow to Obama's policies emanated from a poll question about settlements[211]: "Do you agree or disagree with the Obama administration's call for a stop to all new Israeli settlement construction?" the survey asked. The outcome: 51 percent disagreed; only 41 percent agreed.

This percentage of Jewish opponents ran contrary to Obama's political calculations, as he focused his attention on settlements. His assumption, not an unreasonable one, was simple: American Jews have no desire to see settlement expansion; hence, they are likely to support his demand for settlement freeze. The AJC survey proved Obama and his advisers wrong for one of two reasons: One, Jews don't think what Obama advisers thought they did. In other words, they do not oppose settlements as much as we all believed they do. Or two (and it's the right option to pick), the Obama administration was going much too far with the pressure on Israel, while the Israeli government was much better at explaining why it couldn't go as far as Obama wanted it to. In short, most American Jews still didn't have much sympathy for settlement expansion, but (much like the Israelis) they also didn't understand the rush to push Israel around, and didn't quite see the logic of the uncompromising demand for a "total freeze" at this point in time.

Obama has a two-pronged answer to all suspicions related to his Israel policy, and this has been the case since the early days of his presidential candidacy. On the one hand, he seeks to convince the voters that the eight years under George W. Bush were bad for Israel and that Obama was the change Israel needed.[212] On the other hand, he makes the case that real support of Israel is taking care of its defense, and that Israel's security, as Obama has said many times, is "sacrosanct."[213]

When I interviewed Obama in early 2007,[214] he told me that "the United States' special relationship with Israel obligates us to be helpful to them in the search for credible partners with whom they can make peace, while also supporting Israel in defending itself against enemies sworn to its destruction." In other words, picking a fight with Israel over the peace process is what the United States has to do as a friend — and it also has to take care to keep Israel secure.

It was a risky tactic that didn't always work but has seemingly been finding its audience in recent months. As U.S.-Israel tensions over the Palestinian issue have been swept under the rug for the time being, and Iran tensions more easily relate to the Obama theme of Israel's "defense and security," the president may have found his magic bullet.

This theme of security is driven home at every opportunity. "I made a more full-throated defense of Israel and its legitimate security concerns than any president in history," Obama told interviewer Jeffrey Goldberg in early 2012.[215] Later in the year, when Mitt Romney was in Israel for a visit, Obama ceremoniously signed a U.S.-Israel Enhanced Security Act, saying, "As many of you know, I have made it a top priority for my administration to deepen cooperation with Israel across the whole spectrum of security issues."[216] Obama's campaign adviser and former defense official recently argued[217] that "the case for Obama's Israel policy begins with record-high levels of Foreign Military Financing

(FMF). The Obama administration has increased security assistance to Israel every single year since the president took office, providing nearly $10 billion in aid — covering roughly a fifth of Israel's defense budget — over the past three years."

The list of Obama-induced assistance to Israel's security is indeed very long, as Israeli officials readily admit. When Israeli President Shimon Peres was awarded the Presidential Medal of Freedom by Obama, he included in his speech a line alluding to Obama's record of such support — the line Obama needed for his campaign. "Mr. President," Peres said, "you have pledged a lasting friendship for Israel. You stated that Israel's security is sacrosanct for you. So you pledged; so you act." Even Prime Minister Netanyahu, not Obama's most ardent fan, gave the president his due in an AIPAC speech: "President Obama spoke about his ironclad commitment to Israel's security. He rightly said that our security cooperation is unprecedented … And he has backed those words with deeds."[218]

These statements from Israeli officials, bolstered by numbers and dates and budgetary details, give Obama the case with which to reject the anti-Israel claim, so he believes. Critics think otherwise. They believe that Obama's image as a president who is ready, and even eager, to pick a fight with the Israeli government is already set in stone. And they also believe that Obama's financial and tactical support of Israel's defense does not compensate for the strategic errors made by his administration — or for statements made by some members of the party he represents.

Just as this book was going to print, the Democratic Party, for reasons that are unclear, embarrassed Obama again, making it more difficult for him to present a credible case on Israel.[219] When the Democrats convened in North Carolina for their convention, it was revealed that sections in the party platform having to do with Israel had been changed. Why the change? No one could quite explain it, but the result was disastrous. The Democrats omitted Jerusalem from the platform, no longer affirming it as the capital of Israel; Republicans were quick to seize on this omission and use it for attack; Democrats were defensive, offering different excuses for the omission and eventually caving to pressure, in a questionable vote on the convention floor. Jerusalem is one of the few topics on which American Jews still have something resembling a consensus. In AJC surveys, a 60 percent majority opposes any compromise on the status of Jerusalem. A survey by the dovish J Street found that, "Jerusalem is the one final status issue where American Jews have expressed difficulty reaching a compromise." No wonder, then, that Obama and his political team were pressured. Losing Florida Jews over this uncalled for platform brouhaha was not what they had in mind.

Thus, the next day, the convention was asked, on behalf of the president, to put Jerusalem back into the platform.[220] And not just to put it back but to make it even stronger by advocating for a Jerusalem that "should remain an undivided city." This didn't go through as smoothly as the president's people planned. Delegates protested and booed, proving, yet again, that Israel is becoming a wedge issue. Republicans are using it for attacks; Democrats are getting annoyed by these attacks and reacting accordingly. And poor Obama is stuck in the middle between the Republicans that criticize him, the Democrats that make life harder for him, and the puzzled Jews, wanting to believe him but getting confused by the conflicting messages he sends.

And then there are the Israelis. They are also suspicious of Obama: while his approval numbers in Israel improved from disastrous to mediocre between 2008 and 2012,[221] Israelis would still like Romney to get elected.[222] Why? Jerusalem is a possibility, but the real answer is Iran.

6. The Iran Factor

Israelis never wanted Barack Obama to become the president of the United States.[223] About half of them (49 percent) wanted John McCain to get elected in 2008, compared to 31 percent for Obama. (The rest didn't have an opinion — it was, after all, the American elections, about which not all Israelis need have an opinion). After Obama was elected, a large number of Israelis never approved of the president's Middle East policies, and many considered him to be more or equally "pro-Palestinian" as he is "pro-Israel,"[224] a verdict that is quite harsh. Israelis, for better or worse, expect the American president to be friendly, and had been spoiled in the 16 consecutive years of Presidents Clinton and Bush — both of whom most Israelis considered very friendly. They now expect all future presidents to be like Clinton or Bush.

Obama was eyed more suspiciously. A 2012 survey[225] had found that most Israeli respondents had an "overall favorable opinion of Barack Obama, but are skeptical about his Middle East policies."[226] While Obama is attempting to convince the world that his support for Israel's security is more profound and should be considered of more value than the support Israel received from previous presidents, just 1 percent of Israelis rank him as the "friendliest" president ever (with 59 percent giving Bill Clinton the title and 35 percent awarding it to George W. Bush).[227] When Israelis were asked to comment on Obama's fierce defense of Israel at the United Nations, a vast majority of them said they believed it was all political masquerading — all about Obama "wanting a second term" (76 percent). Just a meager 12 percent thought the motivation behind Obama's United Nations speech was "true friendship."[228]

By early 2012, 69 percent of Israelis were unsatisfied with the way Obama was handling the issue of Iran (compared to just 15 percent who were satisfied). However, this might not mean much. Israelis, by and large, are understandably confused by the Iran debate. In the aforementioned 2012 poll, 45 percent of them supposedly seemed to contradict themselves. On the one hand, they were not satisfied with Obama; on the other hand, they were saying that they believed Obama "will prevent Iran from having nuclear weapons." So why are so many of them not satisfied? At times, it is because they barely know what they want from their own government, let alone the foreign leader of another country. At times, it is because they know exactly what they want, but can't be sure their wishes are actually realistic.

Since Israelis don't believe in the feasibility of diplomatic prevention (as Americans do), what they want from Obama is for the United States to take part in a war of prevention against Iran. In all polls in which the option of an American-backed attack was presented to Israeli respondents, the number of those supporting a do-it-yourself attack significantly diminishes. In a poll of 500

Israelis by Shibley Telhami of the Saban Center for Middle East Policy at the Brookings Institution, 34 percent of respondents opposed any strike against Iran's nuclear facilities, but some 42 percent backed an attack "only if Israel gains at least American support" (19 percent were for striking alone).[229] In a study by Camil Fuchs, professor of statistics at Tel Aviv University, 58 percent of respondents said Israel should not attack without the United States (26 percent said it should regardless of U.S. support). A Channel 2 News poll put at 65 percent the figure of Israelis who oppose going it alone.[230]

In choosing the middle option — yes to an attack, but only with U.S. participation or support — Israelis react to poll questions much like Americans do under similar circumstances.[231] In 2012, American polls concerning Iran followed two possible patterns: When presented with various options for halting Iran's nuclear program, more Americans reasonably chose the less violent option. Thus, when an option such as "diplomacy" or "sanctions" was available to respondents, they tended to go for this middle-of-the-road choice.[232] However, when Americans were presented with only two options, learning to live with a nuclearized Iran or attacking it to prevent it from meeting this goal, they tended to support an attack (but not as consistently). One example: In 2011, a poll by the German Marshall Fund presented Americans (and Europeans) with two options: to take "military action against Iran" or to "simply accept that Iran could acquire nuclear weapons." Presented with such a binary scenario, 49 percent of Americans (and as many as 42 percent of Europeans) opted for the violent option.

In both cases, the American polls and the Israeli polls, the ambivalence of respondents reflected the instinctive understanding that war with Iran should not be desired, as well as the natural tendency of respondents to look for more advantageous measures to prevent Iran from having nuclear weapons. For Israelis, the better measure was the involvement of the United States.[233] Many of them understood that Israel can "delay" but not "destroy" the Iranian nuclear program — as the U.S. Chairman of the Joint Chiefs of Staff publicly explained.[234] And thus, Israel's long summer of Iran-debate[235] was really not a debate between supporters and opponents of an aggressive move by Israel, but more a debate over the best way to make the Americans commit to this effort.

* * *

In 2004, just before the Bush-Kerry election, a survey conducted by 10 newspapers around the world had revealed that Israelis were the public most supportive of the U.S. war in Iraq.[236] Almost 70 percent of Israelis were — at the time — still supportive of the war, which doesn't even present the full picture, given that most opponents of the war were Israeli Arabs. In other words, the only reason there was not wall-to-wall support for the war among Israel's citizens "is the fact that around

65 percent of Israeli Arabs believe that the U.S. invasion was not justified and only 25 percent believe it was."[237] Israeli Jews were almost unanimous (Jews can never be truly unanimous, can they?) in their support of the war.

I have a slide with the results of this long-forgotten poll that I often use in lectures I give on the differences between Israeli Jews and American Jews. And another slide follows it: one with which I present the percentage of American Jews who were supportive of the war at about the same time the Israeli poll was taken. American Jews, according to a Gallup analysis, were the least likely group to support the Iraq war.[238] And Gallup's data was consistent with many other polls that carried the same message, such as the 2005 American Jewish Committee annual survey of Jewish opinion, according to which 70 percent of Jews disapproved of the war; and the one of 2003, when most Americans still supported the war, in which 54 percent of Jews already disapproved of it. Moreover, Jewish opposition wasn't just a matter of party affiliation — not just the tendency of Jewish Americans to vote Democratic and oppose all Republican policies. "Jewish war opposition goes beyond their basic political leanings. Jewish people are more likely to oppose the war than non-Jews of the same political persuasion," explained the Gallup analysis. Comparing Jewish to non-Jewish Democrats, it was revealed that 89 percent of the former opposed the war, compared with 78 percent of the latter.

These two slides — Jewish Israeli and Jewish American opinion on the war —generate a textbook mirror image:

almost 80 percent of Jewish Israelis support the war, while almost 80 percent (77 percent, to be precise) of Jewish Americans oppose it. Israeli Jews, when it comes to the Iraq war, were more in line with American Mormons than with American Jews. For anyone to presume that American Jews might support an American war, or might urge an American president to support one, just because Israelis see it as beneficial would be a mistake, as the Iraq war clearly proved.

Most American Jews did not appreciate the war and did not support its instigator. They did not vote for George W. Bush in the first place. But their growing dislike of him ultimately created one of those bizarre anomalies that characterize current relations between the two largest Jewish communities — another mirror image: The Jews of Israel comprised perhaps the most sympathetic group toward Bush in the entire world. They were certainly more supportive of him than the general American public, and may very well have been more sympathetic to him than any particular group of Americans. On the other hand, American Jews constituted one of the least sympathetic groups toward Bush. A vast majority of them opposed Bush. Indeed, many truly loathed him.[239] For those, digesting a reality in which an Israeli prime minister stands at Bush's side and describes the war in Iraq as an achievement was not easy to swallow. In fact, Israeli fondness for Bush probably served to alienate American Jews from Israel.

Enter the 2012 Iran.

Iran is not Iraq. It is more dangerous, as most Americans believe.[240] It is dangerous to Israel and to the United States, as the Obama administration says. On Iran, Republicans and Democrats used different tones and had somewhat different policy positions, but both opposed the nuclearization of Iran, and both, at least rhetorically, were leaving "all options on the table," including war. Democrats, at least in public, have never said that war with Iran is inconceivable.

What if the Iranians would not talk and would not comply with U.N. resolutions? In a speech at an Israeli conference in 2007, Democratic candidate John Edwards said, "Let me be clear: Under no circumstances can Iran be allowed to have nuclear weapons. … We need to keep all options on the table. Let me reiterate — all options must remain on the table."[241] A couple of weeks later, Hillary Clinton said, "No option can be taken off the table" and "we cannot, we should not, we must not permit Iran to build or acquire nuclear weapons." Obama, before becoming president, when he was not even a candidate, was even more blunt. "In light of the fact that we're now in Iraq, with all the problems in terms of perceptions about America that have been created, us launching some missile strikes into Iran is not the optimal position for us to be in," Obama told the Chicago Tribune in 2004. "On the other hand," he added, "having a radical Muslim theocracy in possession of nuclear weapons is worse. So I guess my instinct would be to err on not having those weapons in the possession of the ruling clerics of Iran."

* * *

Obama has changed his views on Iran more than once in recent years.[242] And there was good news and bad news associated with this change of position. The good news was that Obama appeared serious enough to change his position when he was clearly wrong: "There's no reason why we would necessarily meet with [Iran's President Mahmoud] Ahmadinejad before we know that he was actually in power. He's not the most powerful person in Iran," Obama said in May of 2008. This was a positive 180-degree change from saying, not much earlier, that he would be meeting the president of Iran.

The bad news: the original misstatement, when Obama vowed to meet with Ahmadinejad, should never have taken place. It appended and raised the suspicion that Obama, first, did not have the necessary experience to be commander in chief (a worry that is no longer valid in 2012); second, that Obama had the wrong gut feeling when it came to issues of national security (a suspicion that is still being raised, as many Republicans would be more than eager to demonstrate); and third, that Obama was being calculatedly dishonest about Iran for political reasons (a suspicion that is the most troubling today, as Election Day is getting closer, and Iran tensions are getting higher by the day).[243]

The story of the Obama flip-flop on Iran is a little confusing, but to examine the still-relevant suspicions mentioned above, it is worth repeating. During the fourth Democratic debate of the previous campaign — Charleston, South Carolina, July 2007 — Obama was asked this question[244]: "Would you be willing to meet separately, without precondition, during the first year of your administration, in Washington or anywhere else, with the leaders of Iran, Syria, Venezuela, Cuba and North Korea, in order to bridge the gap that divides our countries?"

Obama's response was unequivocal: "I would. And the reason is this, that the notion that somehow not talking to countries is punishment to them — which has been the guiding diplomatic principle of this administration — is ridiculous."

Technically speaking, Obama was not promising a meeting with Ahmadinejad, but with "the leaders" of Iran and the other countries mentioned. Later, when he was accused of backtracking, Obama argued, parsing his own words, that Ahmadinejad "is not the most powerful person in Iran," in which case he is not the leader, in which case when Obama vowed to meet with "the leaders" he did not really intend to meet with the president of Iran. This was a crafty explanation, albeit a clearly dishonest one. For almost a year, from July of 2007 to March of 2008, the impression was that Obama did intend to meet with Ahmadinejad, and Obama did not make any visible effort to correct this impression. That is, until he did.

The issue of Iran came back to life and spawned a barrage of attacks on Obama in the spring of 2008. In a speech President Bush made in Israel — the "appeasement speech" — he likened "those who would negotiate with 'terrorists and radicals' to appeasers of the Nazis."[245] Without ever mentioning Obama by name, Bush was implicitly criticizing his position of engagement with Iran in the harshest terms available. "As Nazi tanks crossed into Poland in 1939," Bush said, "an American senator declared: 'Lord, if only I could have talked to Hitler, all of this might have been avoided.' We have an obligation to call this what it is — the false comfort of appeasement, which has been repeatedly discredited by history."[246] And of course, these remarks did not go unanswered. Comments from all prospective candidates on the wisdom of meeting with the rogue leaders of rogue states followed, including a response from the man at the center of this debate, Obama: "Instead of tough talk and no action, we need to do what Kennedy, Nixon and Reagan did and use all elements of American power — including tough, principled and direct diplomacy — to pressure countries like Iran and Syria. George Bush knows that I have never supported engagement with terrorists," Obama responded.

Essentially, Obama's problem was not political. It was the fact that he was wrong on the merits. Obama, argued some commentators — notably Charles Krauthammer[247] — was caught unprepared in the debate of 2007, and "after that, there was no going back. So he doubled down. What started as a gaffe became policy. By now, it has become doctrine. Yet it is today what it was on the day he blurted it out: an absurdity."

An absurdity it was, and Obama's aides were trying to help him out of the miserable mistake.[248] They said he was "misunderstood." Then Obama's adviser, Susan Rice, was "channeling Bill Clinton," as Kimberly Strassel described it, when she attempted to parse the "leader" line, arguing that "he said he'd meet with the appropriate Iranian leaders. He hasn't named who that leader will be." Tom Daschle, another Obama ally, was trying another Clintonesque explanation: "It's important to emphasize, again, when we talk about preconditions we're just saying everything needs to be on the table. I would not say that we would meet unconditionally."

The funny thing about all this is that Obama, not long before the 2007 debate in which he stated the position from which he had to climb down, actually gave the right answer on Iran in an interview I had with him.[249] I asked Obama whether the United States should talk with Tehran while the centrifuges are still spinning and producing more enriched uranium, and Obama's answer was both a yes and a no: "It's important to have low-level talks" with Iran even without them freezing the enrichment," he said. However, high-level talks "will not be appropriate without some sense of progress" on the enrichment issue. Namely, no preconditions for low-level talks, preconditions for meeting with the "leaders," whoever they might be.

At the end of this long saga, Obama was inching backward as fast as a candidate can in this era of "gotcha" politics. He was trying to distance himself from his previously stated position without losing his air of dignity.

* * *

Would Obama be willing to use all necessary means to stop Iran? In 2012 we are way beyond the theoretical question of "engagement." Obama tried, failed, changed course and imposed severe sanctions. Let us briefly examine his foreign policy record: On the one hand, there are his repeated attempts to engage Muslim and Arab countries, not always bearing fruit. On the other hand, there is his uncompromising approach to killing terrorists, especially in the Afghanistan-Pakistan region. Obama ordered the assassination of Osama Bin Laden and got credit for it from both political friends and foes. He supported and orchestrated American involvement in the war to topple Libya's Muammar Khadafy, leading it, as critics are always happy to remind, "from behind." He abandoned Egypt's Hosni Mubarak and decided not to intervene in Syria. He made good (or bad) on his pledge to pull America away from the wars in Iraq and Afghanistan. In short, he has a mixed record, about which the public seems quite comfortable: Obama's approval ratings in foreign policy are much better than in other areas.

The question now is whether sanctions will suffice to make Iran cave. In the months leading to the beginning of the official campaign, warnings from Israel were stark, and the attempt by the Obama administration to convince Israel to patiently wait for the sanctions to work was also clearly visible.

Whether Israel should attack Iran or not is not an easy question to answer. As this book is written an attack has not been yet launched; what happens after the book is released is beyond prediction.

While the public gets to hear the conflicting views of officials and former officials on the matter, it doesn't have the required information with which to form an opinion that carries much weight.[250] This is, of course, problematic. On the one hand, one has to wonder: Why is it that the Israeli military establishment is up in arms against an imminent attack? What do they know that we don't? Would we have a better way of assessing the situation if we knew what "they" know? To form an opinion on this matter, one must delve into a couple of crucial questions.

Clearly it is better for the world and the region if Iran does not have nuclear weapons. Very few people would argue that an Iran with nuclear capability would actually contribute to global stability (there are, in fact, very few such people). However, assuming that a nuclearized Iran is dangerous, one still has to contemplate the following: How dangerous, and dangerous to whom? Is it dangerous enough to justify a long and very costly war? There are many dangerous threats, but not all justify such action. Thus, one has to try and assess these two questions: First, will the future damage caused by a nuclear Iran be much greater than the damage of an imminent war? Second, how likely is it that such damage would materialize? An imminent war is, well, imminent. But a future danger is fuzzier. Should Israel go to war now because of a danger that may or may not not occur later?

It is reasonable to assume that if Iran is mostly dangerous to Israel, Israel will be the one most eager to take military action against Iran. The United States is Israel's ally, but that doesn't mean it will go to war for something that is not a crucial American interest. As Israel contemplated Obama's urging for a delay of military action, it had to consider the possibility that for Obama, Iran might never be urgent enough to launch a war, that he might change his position on the severity of the threat the way he changed his position on meeting with the president of Iran.

In recent months, the Israeli government has been consistently declaring that the range of sanctions against Iran is a failure and that while Iran is hurting, it is not getting any closer to caving. In fact, Israel has been saying that while the world is busy with employing more sanctions and feeling good about doing something, the Iranians are moving forward with their program.

Some Israeli and other international players are more hopeful about the sanctions. They can't yet say that sanctions are working since the Iranians haven't yet caved under the pressure, but people around the world (and some in Israel as well) do believe that the current course of nonviolent coercion might lead to a breakthrough. So the obvious question is: Can the combination of tough sanctions and tough talk stop Iran? And this isn't the only question. One should also consider the ticking clock as the wait for sanctions to do the trick continues. In other words, does Israel have time to wait for the sanctions to work? Clearly, Israel's clock is ticking faster than that of the Americans. While the United States might have the time to wait, and only act in the case of ultimate failure of sanctions, Israel — with its smaller military and more limited resources — might not have that luxury. Hence the apprehension, which is exacerbated by Israeli lack of trust in Obama.

Thus, another question comes to the fore: Can Israel forget about its problematic clock if the United States guarantees that no matter what happens, no matter what other countries might be saying, no matter what the circumstances might be, American force will prevent a nuclear Iran? Clearly, there are three problems with such a guarantee: One, no American leader would give such a promise; two, Israel has no way of making sure such a promise is fulfilled (bluntly put, it has no way of punishing America if the promise is broken); and three, Israel has clarified time and again in words and deeds that it will never subcontract its essential security. (On the other hand, Israel constantly relies on American support for its security, so maybe the we-will-defend-ourselves mantra is no more than empty bravado?)

Would Israel change its habitual behavior and have faith in the pledge of an American president? And what if Israelis deem this president untrustworthy? Does it matter if it is a President Obama or a candidate Romney who makes such a promise?

Any promise of commitment can take many forms. It can be a commitment to act or a commitment to stop Iran or a commitment not to interfere with Israeli action (or to support it) or not to reprimand Israel for any action it might take. As one ponders the question of military capabilities, one has to think not just about the initial attack but also the aftermath: Does Israel base its post-strike planning on the assumption that the United States will be joining the battle later in the game, to defend Israel, but also to prevent Iran from rebuilding its sites? And what happens if the United States refuses to play such a role?

Would the United States be satisfied with denouncing Israel, or would it retaliate in some way? A lot depends on the outcome of an Israeli attack. If it's very successful and no harm is done to American interests, one could probably expect the admiration of most Americans. However, if it goes badly and if American interests are hurt and if the crisis drags the economy down without the benefit of having tamed Iran, the damage to the relations could be serious.

And that's why no serious discussion of the Jewish politics of the American 2012 election can be complete without some consideration of the Iran factor.

* * *

Iran is one of the topics with which the Republican candidate could have hoped to sway American Jewish opinion away from Obama. In Romney's version of events, Obama confuses aggressor and victim, and is pressuring Israel to refrain from attacking Iran rather than offering support. "It is sometimes said that those who are the most committed to stopping the Iranian regime from securing nuclear weapons are reckless and provocative and inviting war," Romney said in his speech in Jerusalem in midsummer. "The opposite is true."[251] Without committing to future policies — Romney is a cautious candidate — his message to Jewish Americans concerning Iran is clear: you can't trust the man who already threw Israel "under the bus" on as crucial a matter as Iran.

Fifty-six percent of Jewish Americans said in early 2012 that they are "very concerned" with "the prospect of Iran obtaining nuclear weapons."[252] Thirty-seven percent of respondents also said that they "disapprove" of Obama on this matter — a fairly high number for a relatively Democratic group — and the same percentage said that the Republican Party is "more likely to make the right decision" on Iran. American Jews seem skeptical about the ability of sanctions and diplomacy to achieve success, and 64 percent said they'd support "military action against Iran to prevent it from developing nuclear weapons," should diplomacy fail. (In another poll, 59 percent agreed to military action in the event of diplomatic failure.[253]) As with most such issues, Jews trending Republican tend to support an attack more than Democratic Jews, and they are also those most concerned with Iran and those who have the least confidence in Obama.

But can Iran really be the key with which Romney can take support away from Obama? Some additional information needs to be considered before reaching such a conclusion. The first piece: Only a meager 4 percent of American Jews listed Iran as their most important voting issue, with 15 percent listing it as first, second or third priority. This means that only about one quarter of those proclaiming to be very concerned about Iran would be willing to put their ballot where their mouth is, and vote for the man — be it Obama or Romney — they deem more suitable to deal with Iran.

But even for those convinced when the poll was taken, or who are becoming more convinced since, that Iran should be a top voting issue, the debate over Iran is probably baffling. Assuming they support an Israeli attack, do they support it now? Assuming they don't believe in sanctions, would they scrap this attempt even before Election Day? Assuming they would like to cast their vote for the American candidate who is more likely to make the right decision on Iran, what is the right decision? Even from Israel, the message is far from being clear. The government seems to be saying one thing, while President Shimon Peres is saying something else entirely.[254] This leaves all interpretations of policy viable. If one wants to be reassured that voting for Obama is voting for the right policy on Iran, one can easily find an American or an Israeli expert making this exact argument. If one wants to be persuaded that only a Romney presidency and policy can stop Iran's nuclear race, one can also easily find the experts to support this completely opposite view.

Iran is unlikely to be a game changer, then, unless it is attacked before November — if Israel decides to forgo the Obama advice and go it alone, forcing a burning Middle East on the conscience of the American voter. But even then, how such a move would influence voters is far from clear: Will it make Obama look bad, or prophetic? Will it force him into supporting Israel and silence all critics arguing that he isn't supportive enough? Will it have any influence on Jewish voters? Should it?

Epilogue: Obama or Romney?

In 2007, Barack Obama and Mitt Romney were two of the many presidential candidates to be asked by the prestigious Foreign Policy Magazine to share their thoughts on America's foreign affairs with the magazine readers.[255] Later, it became clear that the Obama article was the more significant, as he became his party nominee for the top job and, later still, the president — while Romney remained on the sidelines before running again, more successfully.

Reading these articles again four years later, one can examine the differences between the candidates with a fresh outlook.

Obama mentioned Israel six times in his article.[256] "Changing the dynamic in Iraq will allow us to focus our attention and influence on resolving the festering conflict between the Israelis and the Palestinians," he wrote, "a task that the Bush administration neglected for years." Romney's article[257] mentioned Israel eight times. "I recently had the privilege of spending some time with Shimon Peres, the former prime minister of Israel," Romney bragged.

Comparing the visions of these two candidates from back then can be entertaining. What a remarkable difference between the two articles: One was about peace, the other about war. One was optimistic, almost upbeat (some would prefer naive and delusional), the other much more pessimistic and grim (some would call it realistic). Obama, in his article, used the word "peace" almost twice as much as Romney (13 to 7). The Republican talked more about "struggle" (5 to 2) and "war" (26 to 13 mentions) and about "challenge" (24 to 7 in Obama's article). But both agreed: America has a big role to play in the region, a leader's role.

Obama did not sound very hopeful on Iran: "We must develop a strong international coalition to prevent Iran from acquiring nuclear weapons," he wrote. Both were promising to maintain and to build alliances. "We need to strengthen old partnerships and alliances and inaugurate new ones to meet twenty-first-century challenges," Romney wrote. Obama couldn't agree more: "I intend to rebuild the alliances, partnerships, and institutions necessary to confront common threats and enhance common security."

Indeed, different articles, different candidates, but separating real differences from the imaginary is an important ingredient of a voter's rational choice. And with Jewish voters, an interesting mirror image campaign is in play.

The Republicans would like Jewish voters to believe that the differences between Obama and Romney on most economic issues are as not as stark as the other side portrays them. When it comes to the economy, the Republicans emphasize not ideology but rather aptitude. The story that the Jews are getting from Romney emissaries is this: He will not take your benefits away, he will not touch the social programs you like so much — at least not now. The elderly Jewish voters of Florida, where Jews might really count, ought not have a Romney-Ryan phobia. The reform that Republicans are talking about is one that will only have an impact on younger generations, not them. And in the meantime, electing Romney will have the advantage of putting a capable manager in control of the economy.

The mirror image is how Democrats talk about the candidates and Israel. *They* would like Jewish voters to believe that the differences between Obama and Romney on Israel are as not as stark as the other side portrays them. When it comes to U.S.-Israel relations, a matter of importance for some Jewish Floridians, the Democrats emphasize not ideology but rather aptitude. The story that the Jews are getting from the Obama emissaries is this: He will not abandon Israel; he will never abandon Israel. True, differences of opinion were highlighted by the media and gave some the impression that the Obama administration is not supportive of Israel. But don't look at his supposed views — look at the president's record. He is giving Israel more military assistance than ever before. He defended Israel at the United Nations, preventing the Palestinians from circumventing direct talks. He amassed an unprecedented coalition to sanction Iran and is putting on the pressure to get even more sanctions in place.

Simply put: Republicans want you to think that, rhetoric aside, Romney is a pragmatic manager of the economy, while Democrats claim that he is an ideologue tilting against your most sacred beliefs. Democrats want you to think that, rhetoric aside, Obama is a pragmatic defender of Israel, while Republicans claim that he is an ideologue tilting against your most sacred beliefs.

Are they right? Are they wrong?

* * *

In the previous chapter, we described in some detail Obama's about-turn on Iran engagement. But Romney also has a long history of — your choice — changing his mind or flip-flopping[258] on a whole set of social issues. Take abortion. Abortion is an issue on which Jewish voters have the most permissive views in the nation. "About twice as many Jews as other Americans believe that abortion should be legal in all cases."[259] Forty-five percent believe abortion should be legal in "all" cases, and another 44 percent believe it should be legal in "most" cases (leaving very few anti-abortion Jewish voters). Should Romney be considered a candidate who is unacceptable, given his views on abortion? That depends on the extent to which one takes seriously the candidate's party platform (staunchly anti-abortion), the candidate's campaign-tailored position ("I'm in favor of abortion being legal in the case of rape and incest, and the health and life of the mother"[260]), Romney's sister's assurances ("He's not going to be touching any of that."[261]

), or Romney's past statements — the ones he was making while running for governor of the blue state of Massachusetts ("I will preserve and protect a woman's right to choose"[262]).

The question is whether Romney has truly changed his mind, in which case he is definitely ideologically to the right of most Jewish voters, or whether he is just masquerading his true feelings for political considerations (not a noble position, but one that politicians are forced to take from time to time). However, what his current position makes clear is this: whether you believe him to be telling the truth or not, abortion is not an issue on which a President Romney is going to spend much of his time. That's essentially the pragmatic argument Jewish voters hear from Republicans on the economy — don't look to the ideology, look to the probable actions. Romney will not erase Medicare for today's elderly, and he will not try to change the rules on abortion, no matter what his views truly are.

With Romney's views on Israel one gets — yet again — the mirror image we keep coming back to. Romney wants Jewish voters to consider differences between him and Obama as minor as possible regarding abortion, but he wants the same voters to consider differences between him and Obama as significant as possible regarding Jerusalem. And he wants to create the impression that he is "better" on Iran, namely, that he is the more trustworthy candidate when it comes to halting Iran's nuclear program. Iran is the only significant "foreign" and "security-related" topic on the agenda on which there's a meaningful gap between Obama-leaning voters and Romney-leaning voters.[263] So for him, toughness and poise on Iran is not just a Jewish issue.

But would a President Romney really be more inclined to be tough on Iran, to use force against Iran? Maybe in his heart Romney feels stronger about Iran than Obama, but publicly he gave little reason to suspect that his policies vis-à-vis Iran would be any different from Obama's.[264] In fact, most everything that Romney says about Iran is mere repetition and repackaging of the current American position. When he was interviewed by Ari Shavit of Ha'aretz, Romney said that an American military strike on Iran's nuclear facilities "should not be ruled out" if other preventive measures fail. He added, "I am personally committed to take every step necessary to prevent Iran from developing a nuclear weapons capability."[265] So Romney doesn't "rule out" a military strike. That's also Obama's position.[266]

That Romney doesn't stray much from the current American position isn't as surprising as some people might think because, at the time of the quoted interview, the stated American position on Iran was very similar to Israel's position. Both countries agreed that an Iranian regime with nuclear weapons is unacceptable; that containment is not a viable option with Iran; that stopping Iran by diplomatic means is preferable to using the military option; and that the military option should remain on the table. Romney, while projecting toughness, did not advocate an abandonment of the diplomatic course and a launching of an American attack. He did not set a date for such an attack. He did not draw any red line, beyond which an attack should be launched — the kind of red line that Israel's prime minister would like Obama to draw.[267]

On Iran, as on many other Israel-related issues, the only real difference isn't a difference between Obama and Romney, it is a difference in the way some senior Israelis are reading the candidates. It is the difference between hearing Obama saying that a nuclearized Iran is unacceptable, and not believing he really means it — and hearing Romney saying the exact same words, and believing him. Naturally, American Jewish voters might decide that Obama is actually the more believable of the two. ⏏

* * *

It was two days before Obama was elected president when I had a couple of hours to kill after his final Ohio rally, 80,000 strong, in downtown Cleveland. So I took the short drive to James Garfield's house, nicely preserved but gloomily deserted. I reminded myself of one of Garfield's quotes: "Few men in our history have ever obtained the presidency by planning to obtain it." Garfield, the twentieth president of the United States, was definitely not planning ahead when he was elected to the highest office in 1880, and quite obviously did not plan his term to end as it did: Garfield was killed by an unstable assassin.

In the long history of campaign political gaffes, a place should be reserved for Garfield's wife, Lucretia. As Kenneth D. Ackerman tells her story in the book about Garfield's life and career,[268] the campaign hadn't even begun when the wife, unaware of a reporter in the friendly crowd in a nearby Ohio town, took a question about "Garfield's role in funding a local anti-drink crusade." The general, she responded, "does not believe in total abstinence. Oh, no! he believes every man should have a mind of his own, but not drink to excess." The newsman's report, writes Ackerman, descended like a "bombshell among the zealous and highly organized Temperance movement."

Incidents such as this one are as common as balloons and hotdogs in the course of every campaign season. Candidates have to hide their true positions from the angry mob, but tiredness and the intensity of the campaign occasionally make them err, and mistakenly share with the public true feelings, such as: "I like being able to fire people who provide services to me"[269] (Romney) or "If you've got a business, you didn't build that"[270] (Obama). When one ponders one's choice — one's vote — one has to separate image from reality to differentiate between campaign slogans and actual policies that the candidate is likely to pursue. In the case of 2012 Obama, that's easier: we already have four years of experience with the president, good and bad. With candidate Romney the task is trickier. Is he a moderate in the closet, a man who does not truly believe in "total abstinence," or a born-again ideologue, who is going to follow every point of the plans laid out in detail in his party's platform?

Three stages of deliberation are essential for the undecided Jewish voter — for every voter really — before making up one's mind (that is, for those wanting to make a rational choice). Three stages that have nothing to do with either Obama or Romney, stages that apply to every candidate in every election in every country.

The first stage is setting an agenda: What are the most important issues before the voters? What are the most crucial issues on which to base one's decision of whom to support? In 2012, as we've shown, most voters — Jews included — consider the American economic situation as the most crucial issue of the day. So one has to ask oneself: Is this really the most important issue for me? Are there other important issues? Are these other issues important enough for me to eventually vote for the candidate less equipped to deal with the American economy? If no issue is more important than the economy, and no issue can make you vote for the lesser economically fit candidate, then you have one problem solved. All you have to do is pick the candidate that you deem better for pulling the economy out of the ditch. If, on the other hand, there are issues that might make you pick the lesser economically fit candidate, you have to figure out what those issues might be and put them in order of importance.

Of course, to do that you have to move to the second stage of deliberation. What exactly would you want the policy to be on this most important issue or issues? Do you want the economy to be saved by raising taxes or by cutting the budget? Do you want more jobs to be added to the market by making the government hire more federal employees, or do you want these jobs added by reducing the burden of taxes on private sector employers? In stage one the voter sets the agenda; in stage two the voter forms policy preferences on the highest agenda items.

Stage three is the one in which a voter looks at the candidates and makes a decision based on the answer to a simple question: of the two candidates, Obama and Romney, which one would pursue the policies that I want on the issues that I most care about?

All other considerations are mere distractions.

Author Information

Shmuel Rosner is the Senior Political Editor for the Jewish Journal, and and writes the influential daily blog Rosner's Domain. He is also a senior fellow at The Jewish People Policy Institute (JPPI); the non-fiction chief editor for Israel's largest Publishing House,Kinneret-Zmora-Bitan-Dvir.

He writes weekly for The International Herald Tribune \ New York Times and for Israel's Maariv Daily (Hebrew). He has written for Slate, Foreign Policy, Commentary, The New Republic, Haaretz, The Jerusalem Post, and others.

Rosner's book *Shtetl Bagel Baseball, on the Wonderful Dreadful State of American Jews* was published in Israel by Keter (Hebrew, 2011) and became a bestseller in Israel.

You can follow him at jewishjournal.com/rosnersdomain and on Twitter @rosnersdomain. His e-mail is rshmuel@gmail.com.

Acknowledgments

The idea for writing this book was Rob Eshman's. Blame him. And blame David Suissa — for shrewdly luring me into the Jewish Journal's orbit.

I wouldn't have been able to complete this book on such a tight schedule without the huge help that I get daily from the Rosner's Domain content editor, Sara Miller. She is doing the work for which I get the credit (of course, errors are mine, not hers).

My friends Prof. Peter Berkowitz, Prof. Yehudah Mirsky and Dr. Shlomo Fischer gave me their thorough advice and, more importantly, their unvarnished opinion.

To the many experts and researchers on whose work I rely in this book and in other endeavors, I owe greatly. I cannot name them all, but you'll be able to find their names and works by looking at the many endnotes to this short volume. It should be noted that in writing this book, I relied heavily on previous work that I've done for the Jewish Journal, but also on my work for other publications, among them Haaretz, the Jerusalem Post, The International Herald Tribune, Slate, Commentary, Foreign Policy, and the New Republic. I thank the editors and other staff members of these publications for assisting me with polishing my initial reporting.

Having to simultaneously juggle my many assignments and the speedy writing of this book during August, I was not much of a husband and father in recent weeks. To my wife, Orna, and my children, Shaul, Yochai, Ariel and Yael, I owe my apologies and my gratitude.

References and Notes

[1] See: 2003 Annual Survey of American Jewish Opinion, the American Jewish Committee. More about this issue in chapter six.

[2] 2000 Annual Survey of American Jewish Opinion, the American Jewish Committee.

[3] The numbers here are taken from: Jewish American Voting Behavior, 1972–2008: Just The Facts, The Solomon Project, Mark S. Mellman, Aaron Strauss, Kenneth D. Wald, 2012. In the Jewish Voting Record, The Jewish Virtual Library, numbers are different: 80 percent for Clinton in 1992, 78 percent for Clinton in 1996, 79 percent for Gore in 2000 (http://www.jewishvirtuallibrary.org/jsource/US-Israel/jewvote.html).

[4] Just The Facts, The Solomon Project.

[5] See: Young Jewish Adults in the United States Today, Ukeles Associates, 2006, page 2.

[6] Ukeles, page 27.

[7] Ukeles, page 72.

[8] Ukeles, page 27.

[9] Comparisons of Jewish Communities, A Compendium of Tables and Bar Charts, Ira Sheskin, 2012.

10 Haaretz, Shmuel Rosner, 2.1.2008.

11 Santorum Wins Iowa, Officially, The Politico, 20.1.2012.

12 See NJPS 2001: http://www.jewishdatabank.org/NJPS2000.asp.

13 See: Estimating the Jewish Population of the United States: 2000-2010, Elizabeth Tighe, Leonard Saxe, Charles Kadushin.

14 See: http://www.jewishdatabank.org/Reports/Jewish_Population_in_the_United_States_2011.pdf.

15 See: The Jewish Vote, Ira Sheskin, 2012.

16 The percentage of households that are Jewish in New York City increased from 15 percent in 2002 to 16 percent in 2011, according to the Jewish Community Study of New York: 2011.

17 Jewish Population in the United States, 2011, Sheskin, Dashefsky.

18 See: The New York Times Election Results, Pennsylvania 2008 http://elections.nytimes.com/2008/results/states/pennsylvania.html

19 See 7, Sheskin.

20 Jewish Issues, Jewish Votes, Mik Moore, Sh'ma, January 2012.

21 The following paragraphs rely heavily on: Jewish Journal, Shmuel Rosner, 7.5.2012 (So, how many Jews will vote for Mitt Romney?).

[22] Haaretz, Shmuel Rosner, 6.19.2008.

[23] See: Presidential Campaigns, Paul F. Boller Jr., Revised Edition, P. 294.

24 Haaretz, Shmuel Rosner, 10.23.2008.

25 Quinnipiac, 10.23.2008: http://www.quinnipiac.edu/institutes-and-centers/polling-institute/presidential-swing-states-(fl-oh-and-pa)/release-detail?ReleaseID=1223.

26 As Mitt Romney pursues must-win Florida, Jewish vote is key target, Tampa Bay Times, 7.31.2012.

27 The following paragraphs heavily rely on: Jewish Journal, Shmuel Rosner, 7.5.2012 (see: 12).

28 See: Jewish Issues, Jewish Votes.

29 See: Why So Few Jews Vote for Republicans, ABC, Jennifer Rubin, 2.13.2007 http://abcnews.go.com/Politics/story?id=2872816&page=1#.UD5R4Nbibz0.

30 Blow: http://blow.blogs.nytimes.com/2010/08/26/obama-and-the-jews-part-2/

31 See: Finally more clarity: 27%-29% of Jews tilt Republican, Jewish Journal, Shmuel Rosner, 5.2.2012.

32 Our data is all available for Rosner's Domain readers, at the so-called US Jewish Party Identification tracker: http://www.jewishjournal.com/rosnersdomain/category/us_jewish_party-identification. : The data was gathered from the annual survey of American Jewish opinion by the American Jewish Committee (AJC), Gallup polls, the study on Jewish Distinctiveness in America by Tom W. Smith (from 2005 — we needed those to get a glimpse of previous decades) and the Pew

Research Center studies.

33 The AJC survey of 2012 gives us an opportunity to better understand party identification trends among Jewish voters, as it posed two questions that are relevant to this issue. The first is the same one that the AJC survey asked in previous polls: "In politics TODAY, do you consider yourself a Republican, a Democrat, or an Independent?" The second question, though, was new, and it was asked only of Jews who declared themselves independent of party identification: "As of TODAY, do you think of yourself as closer to the Republican Party/Democratic Party?" When we combined the Jews identifying with the parties and those "leaning" toward one of the parties, the AJC numbers came pretty close to those of PEW: 65–68 percent Jewish Democrats, 27–29 percent Jewish Republicans.

34 See: Jewish Vote Not a Problem for Obama, The Forward, Jim Gerstein, 11.14.2011 http://forward.com/articles/145934/jewish-vote-not-a-problem-for-obama/

35 See previous comment: 65% + 27% is 92%, leaving 8% on undecided Jewish voters.

[36] See: Mogul's Latest Foray Courts Jews for the G.O.P., New York Times, 7.25.2012.

[37] Forbes number. See: http://www.forbes.com/profile/sheldon-adelson/

[38] National Jewish Democratic Council Doesn't Speak for Me on Adelson, Alan Dershowitz, Huff Post, 7.6.2012.

[39] See: Jewish Journal, Shmuel Rosner, 8.10.2012.

40 Comparison of income by religion: http://awesome.good.is/transparency/web/1002/almighty-dollar/flat.html

41 A Snapshot of the American Jewish Electorate: 2011 Political Survey, Steven Windmueller.

42 Five Keys To The Jewish Vote, James D. Besser, 8.14.2012.

43 Reliably Democratic, Jewish vote gets Romney eye, AP, 7.27.2012.

44 The Reinvention of an Anti-War Activist, Commentary, 7.23.2012.

45 Arizona's Savvy Israel Ally, Tablet, 5.18.2012.

46 Jewish Journal, Shmuel Rosner, 7.18.2012 (House hopeful Sinema responds to criticism: I will be a strong voice for Israel in Congress).

47 Jewish Journal, Shmuel Rosner, 7.15.2012 (What Congress candidate Sinema's emails reveal about her Israel position)

48 Adult Sinema, The Washington Free Beacon, 4.20.2012.

49 In Ohio, Brown-Mandel U.S. Senate race is among the most expensive, JTA, 7.31.2012.

50 Source: http://www.jewishvirtuallibrary.org/jsource/US-Israel/israelpacs.html

51 See: Jewish Vote Not a Problem for Obama.

52 Rosner's Domain Jewish House and Senate projections tell this story in numbers. See it here: http://www.jewishjournal.com/rosnersdomain/category/house_projection

53 The Jewish Vote in Presidential Elections, Sarna.

54 Contentions, Commentary, Shmuel Rosner, 11.5.2008.

[55] Haaretz, Shmuel Rosner, 3.3.2008.

[56] Patrick Healy, NYT, 3.14.2007.

[57] See: Clinton and Obama Court Jewish Vote, Patrick Healy, New York Times, 3.13.2007 http://www.nytimes.com/2007/03/14/us/14aipac.html

[58] Haaretz, Shmuel Rosner, 3.14.2007.

[59] Clinton, Obama Closely Matched Among Jewish Democrats, Gallup, 3.24.2008.

[60] Obama Beats McCain Among Jewish Voters, Gallup, 5.7.2008.

[61] Haaretz, Shmuel Rosner, 4.24.2008.

[62] Haaretz, Shmuel Rosner, 2.6.2008.

[63] Haaretz, Shmuel Rosner, 2.6.2008 ("The Jewish vote: Obama carried Massachusetts and California").

[64] The most convenient compilation of presidential Jewish vote: Jewish Voting Record: U.S. Presidential Elections, Jewish Virtual Library (http://www.jewishvirtuallibrary.org/jsource/US-Israel/jewvote.html). More updated numbers are in: Jewish American Voting Behavior 1972–2008: Just the Facts, Mark S. Mellman, Aaron Strauss, Kenneth D. Wald, July 2012. The Solomon Project study attributes 67 percent is what to Dukakis.

[65] Jewish Journal, Shmuel Rosner, 6.10.2012 (The June Vote, The Jewish Vote).

[66] Mormons Widely Favor Romney; Jewish Voters Back Obama, Gallup, 6.8.2012.

[67]While most reports put the percentage of 2008 Obama Jewish vote at 78 percent — the percentage found in exit polls at the time — a more detailed and nuanced analysis of the Jewish vote by the Solomon Project revealed that Obama's actual Jewish support was 74 percent. See: Jewish American Voting Behavior 1972-2008: Just the Facts, Mark S. Mellman, Aaron Strauss, Kenneth D. Wald, July 2012.

[68]The Jewish Vote in Presidential Elections, Jonathan Sarna, Shma, January 2012.

[69]When General Grant Expelled the Jews, Jonathan D. Sarna, Nextbook, 2012.

[70]Jewish Journal, Shmuel Rosner, 4.9.2012 (Ulysses Grant and the Jewish vote, and its 2012 parallels).

[71]American Jews and the 2008 Presidential Election: As Democratic and Liberal as Ever?, Steven M. Cohen, Sam Abrams, Judith Veinstein, Berman Jewish Policy Archive at NYU Wagner October 20, 2008.

[72]Workmen's Circle National Poll, Steven M. Cohen, Sam Abrams, 2012.

[73]See: Jewish Journal, US Jewish Party Identification. In: Rosner's Domain, J-Meter (http://www.jewishjournal.com/rosnersdomain/category/us_jewish_party-identification).

[74]Chosen for What? Jewish Values in 2012, Robert P. Jones, Daniel Cox, Public Religion Research Institute, April 2012.

[75]Americans Want Next President to Prioritize Jobs, Corruption, Gallup, 7.30.2012.

[76]Jewish American Voting Behavior 1972–2008: Just the Facts, Mark S. Mellman, Aaron Strauss, Kenneth D. Wald, July 2012.

[77]The Democratic Debate in Cleveland, 2.26.2008. Transcript: http://www.nytimes.com/2008/02/26/us/politics/26text-debate.html?pagewanted=all

[78]The following paragraphs draw heavily from: Haaretz, Shmuel Rosner, 2.27.2008 (**A promise no Jewish liberal can ignore**). A version of the same story is also featured in: Shtetl, Bagel Baseball, On the Dreadful, Wonderful State of American Jews, Shmuel Rosner, Keter, 2011 (Hebrew).

[79]Read more about it in: Troubling the Waters: Black-Jewish Relations in the American Century, Cheryl Lynn Greenberg, Princeton University Press, 2006.

[80]Revisiting the 2008 Presidential Election: Reflections on the Jewish Vote, Steven Windmueller, JCPA, April 2009.

[81]A dual heritage: the public career of Oscar S. Straus, Naomi Wiener Cohen, 1969.

[81]Are American Jews Becoming Republican? Insight into Jewish Political Behavior, Steven Windmueller, JCPA, 2003.

[82]See: American President, A Reference Resource, Oscar S. Straus (1906–1909): Secretary of Commerce and Labor, http://millercenter.org/president/roosevelt/essays/cabinet/1799

[83]Quoted in: Jews in American Politics, At the Summit, David G. Dalin, P. 33.

[84]A dual heritage: the public career of Oscar S. Straus, Naomi Wiener Cohen, 1969.

[85]Are American Jews Becoming Republican? Insight into Jewish Political Behavior, Steven Windmueller, JCPA, 2003.

[86]See: Young people in Israel and in the USA: Using the difference to make a difference, Shmuel Rosner, Dr. Dov Mimon and Inbal Heckman, JPPI, 2012.

[87]The Ten Commandments of America's Jews, Jack Wertheimer, Commentary, June 2012.

[88]Haaretz, Shmuel Rosner, 8.6.2007.

[89]All numbers and sources in this paragraph can be found at Polling Report (http://www.pollingreport.com/health.htm)

[90]Election 2010: Jim McCormick wants your (FL-19, Jewish) vote, Jerusalem Post, Shmuel Rosner, 2.10.2010.

[91]Jewish voters (in FL-19): As Democratic as ever, Jerusalem Post, Shmuel Rosner, 4.17.2010.

[92]A Solomon Project White Paper: The Jewish vote in 2010, the April 13, 2010 special in FL 19.

[93]Fall 2010 Survey of American Jewish Opinion.

[94]2012 AJC Survey of American Jewish Opinion.

[95]For many American Jews, Obama's health care plan is a top cause, The Forward, Nathan Guttman, 12.10.2009.

[96]A Snapshot of the American Jewish Electorate: 2011 Political Survey, Steven Windmueller.

[97]In Wertheimer, see 7.

[98]The Making of the President 1972, Theodor White, 2010 edition, page 120–121.

[99]Jews in American Politics, Maisel and Forman (Eds). The recent study by the Solomon Project put the number at 32 percent, based on the CBS poll.

[100] Jewish American Voting Behavior 1972–2008: Just the Facts, Mark S. Mellman, Aaron Strauss, Kenneth D. Wald, 2012, page 17.

[101]Obama Still Wins on Likability; Romney, on the Economy, Gallup, 8.24.2012.

[102]Pollster.com average, 8.24.2012. This number changes as the polls change; the updated average is here: http://elections.huffingtonpost.com/pollster/obama-job-approval-economy

[103]AJC 2012, see 13.

[104]For an interesting discussion of this question, see the Kol Safran blog: http://kol-safran.blogspot.co.il/2011/07/mistaken-attribution.html

[105]Workmen's Circle / Arbeter Ring 2012 American Jews' Political Values Survey.

[106]Wald's discussion is in: Stunning Stability: A Consistent Jewish Vote for 60 Years, Sh'ma, Keneth D. Wald, January 2012.

[107]How Not to Repair the World, Commentary, Hillel Halkin, July 2008.

[108]Chosen for What, Jewish Values in 2012, Public Religion Research Institute, 2012.

[109]More about this survey: Jewish Journal, Shmuel Rosner, 4.4.2012 (The best representative of American Jewish values (guess who?))

[110] This survey had also some strange results, the most notable of them that most American Jews (61 percent) believe that Israeli Prime Minister Benjamin Netanyahu "well represent[s] Jewish values." But this quirky nugget is no more than a warning sign: if you're looking for consistency in this survey — in all surveys of Jews — you might lose your way.

[111]Contemporary American Judaism, Dana Evan Kaplan, 2009, page 80.

[112]The 'tikkun olam' president, Jerusalem Post, Steven M. Bob, 12.31.2011.

[113]Workmen's Circle, 2012.

[114]Pew, The Complicated Politics of Abortion, 8.22.2012.

[115]More Support for Gun Rights, Gay Marriage than in 2008 or 2004, Pew, 4.25.2012.

[116]Workmen's Circle, 2012.

[117]Obama Gay Marriage Nod Praised By Many Jewish Groups, The Jewish Week, 5.10.2012.

[118]Remarks by the President on the Economy — Cleveland, OH, 6.14.2012.

[119]Obama AP interview. 8.25.2012.

[120]Workmen's Circle, 2012.

[121]Romney Lost the American Jewish Vote by Picking Paul Ryan, Daily Beast, 8.14.2012.

[122]The Fight For the Jewish Vote, Newsweek, 10.10.2008.

[123]Why Jews Hate Palin, Commentary, January 2010.

[124]Haaretz, Shmuel Rosner, 11.1.2006.

[125]Parts of this chapter rely heavily on: Jews and the 2008 Election, Commentary, Shmuel Rosner, February 2009.

[126]Jewish Journal, Shmuel Rosner, 3.21.2012 (Is the US too supportive of Israel? That depends on one's political affiliation).

[127]See 5 for all references and links to the poll sighted in this paragraph.

[128]Jewish Journal, Shmuel Rosner, 7.27.2012.

[129]Americans More Positive Than Negative Toward Netanyahu, Gallup, 7.29.2012.

[130]For this excellent profile of Senor: Romney's Jewish Connector, Tablet, 7.27.2012 (http://www.tabletmag.com/jewish-news-and-politics/107589/romneys-jewish-connector).

[131]The New York Times published a detailed account of the Romney-Netanyahu friendship. See: A Friendship Dating to 1976 Resonates in 2012, NYT, 4.7.2012 (http://www.nytimes.com/2012/04/08/us/politics/mitt-romney-and-benjamin-netanyahu-are-old-friends.html?pagewanted=all).

[132]Reported by: Haaretz, Barak Ravid.

[133]Jewish Journal, Shmuel Rosner, 7.31.2012.

[134]Jerusalem Post, Shmuel Rosner, (The Obama administration was wrong, wrong, wrong on Israel).

[135]See: What's the state of the race in the Illinois 10th? Depends which poll you believe, JTA, 8.20.2012.

[136]Schnider is Jewish, so you can follow the state of the race with our House Jewish tracker (http://www.jewishjournal.com/rosnersdomain/category/house_projection).

[137]UPS suspicious packages contained explosives meant for Chicago houses of worship: law enforcement, NY Daily News, 10.29.2010.

[138]Jewish Journal, Shmuel Rosner, 3.17.2012.

[139] http://www.jweekly.com/article/full/31825/aipac-conference-opens-to-controversy-starting-with-john-hagee/

[140]http://forward.com/articles/140260/christian-pro-israel-group-stakes-claim-on-right/

[141]A word of caution is advised: A member of CUFI only has to sign on and give an active email address — no dues involved.

[142]This is taken from an RJC statement.

[143]See in: Jewish Journal, Shmuel Rosner, 3.21.2012.

[144] See: David Brog on why Christians support the Jewish state, 5.7.2006.

[145]Jewish Journal, Shmuel Rosner, 7.23.2012 (Hagee on stopping Iran, admiring Netanyahu and Obama's Mideast mistake).

[146]See: Are Republicans Ready Now for a Mormon President?, Pew, 7.5.2011.

[147]American Jews and Evangelical Christians: Anatomy of a Changing Relationship, Carl Schrag, Jerusalem Center for Public Affairs (JCPA), 5. 2005.

[148]A Match Made in Heaven, Zev Chafets, 2007.

[149]Haaretz, Shmuel Rosner, 12.31.2006.

[150]The 2012 Jewish Values Survey.

[151]See: The Christian Right in the Presidential Nominating Process, Duane M. Oldfield, In: In Pursuit of the White House, 1996.

[152]Jewish American Voting Behavior, Mellman, Strauss, Wald.

[153]The 2012 Jewish Values Survey.

[154]From a Twitter Photo to Treatment, NYT, 6.11.2011.

[155]Jewish Population Survey of Congressional Districts: 2000 and 2006, David M. Paul, 2009 (http://www.jewishdatabank.org/Archive/N-Congressional_Districts_2000_2006_MainReport.pdf).

[156]Dems' fate in NY special sparks '12 fears, The Hill, 9.13.2011.

[157]See previous note.

[158]Seeing Ripple in Jewish Vote, NYT, 9.14.2011.

[159]Jews and the 2008 Election, Commentary, Shmuel Rosner, 2.2009.

[160]Did Israel, gay marriage or the economy make the difference in GOP's win in N.Y.?, JTA (In: Jewish Journal), 9.14.2011.

[161]Siena Research Institute poll, 9.9.2011.

[162]Race to Replace Weiner Down to the Wire, NYT, 9.7.2011.

[163]See: http://www.realclearpolitics.com/video/2012/08/11/krauthammer_paul_ryan_has_that_reagan-like_quality.html

[164]Fussbudget, The New Yorker, 8.6.2012.

[165]This part of the analysis is borrowed from: Jewish Journal, Shmuel Rosner, 12.23.2011 (Jewish voters and the Ron Paul effect).

[166]Will the Palin Effect Again Cost GOP Among Jewish Voters?, Daily Kos, 9.28.2011.

[167]The Fight for the Jewish Vote, Daily Beast, 10.9.2008.

[168]The quote is of Prof. Kenneth Wald.

[169]2008 Annual Survey of American Jewish Opinion (http://www.ajc.org/site/apps/nlnet/content3.aspx?c=ijITI2PHKoG&b=846741&ct=5989933).

[170]See: Obama Winning Over the Jewish Vote, Gallup, 10.23.2012.

[171]Romney, Ryan and Florida Jews, Jewish Journal, 8.15.2012.

[172]Ryan's Proposals Lack Jewish Values, The Jewish Week, 8.28.2012.

[173]Why Jewish voters will choose Obama over Romney, The Hill, 8.29.2012.

[174]Jewish Journal, David Suissa, 8.15.2012 (Paul Ryan's Courage).

[175]Kennedy Still Highest-Rated Modern President, Nixon Lowest, Gallup, 12.6.2010.

[176]Percentages here are taken from The Solomon Project's Jewish American Voting Behavior. Carter's share of the Jewish vote of a "two party vote" was 54 percent to Reagan's 46 percent.

[177]Jewish American Voting Behavior.

[178]The Jewish Vote in Presidential Elections, Jonathan D. Sarna, Shma, 2012.

[179]The Israel Swing Factor: How the American Jewish Vote Influences U.S. Elections, Jeffrey S. Helmreich, JCPA, 2001.

[180]It should be noted that Carter lost New York in 1976 as well. See: Jimmy Carter and the New York Democrats, NYT, 1.31.2008.

[181]The Palm Beach Post, 8.13.1980.

[182]See: Jeffrey S. Helmreich.

[183]My Problem with Jimmy Carter's Book, Kenneth W. Stein, Middle East Quarterly, 2007.

[184]White House Diary, Jimmy Carter, Farrar, Straus and Giroux, 2010.

[185]Jimmy Carter: Israel's 'apartheid' policies worse than South Africa's, Haaretz, 12.11.2006.

[186]Carter offers Jewish community 'Al Het', Rom Kampeas, JTA, 12.21.2009.

[187]White House pushes back against Suskind book's depiction of Obama and his staff, Mike Allen, Politico, 9.17.2011.

[188]There are many studies chronicling this change in Israel-Diaspora relations. See, for example: Loyalty and Criticism in the Relations between the World Jewry and Israel, Gabriel Sheffer, The Israeli Presidential Conference 2011.

[189]With Jews Like Us, IHT, Shmuel Rosner, 6.28.2012.

[190]Haaretz, Shmuel Rosner, 2.26.2008.

[191]Haaretz, Shmuel Rosner, 1.28.2008.

[192]Haaretz, Shmuel Rosner, 1.25.2008.

[193]Who are you, Barack Obama?, Danny Ayalon, Jerusalem Post.

[194]Haaretz, Shmuel Rosner, 3.18.2008.

[195]Watch it here: http://www.youtube.com/watch?v=AgHHX9R4Qtk

[196]See: Mr. President, Save Your Breath! No Speech for Israel!, Shmuel Rosner, The New Republic, 8.5.2009.

[197]Mitt Romney: Obama threw Israel 'under the bus' in speech, Michael A. Memoli, LA Times, 5.19.2011.

[198]The following paragraphs are based or taken from a long feature piece for Maariv (Hebrew). The full story behind Israel-US ties, Shmuel Rosner, 11.6.2009 (translated by Sara Miller).

[199]Remarks by Obama and Netanyahu, the Oval Office, 5.18.2009 (transcript: http://www.whitehouse.gov/the-press-office/remarks-president-obama-and-israeli-prime-minister-netanyahu-press-availability).

[200]Abbas's Waiting Game on Peace With Israel, Washington Post, Jackson Diehl, 5.29.2009.

[201]US presses Israel on settlements, AlJazeera, 5.20.2009.

[202]The President's Speech in Cairo: A New Beginning (http://www.whitehouse.gov/blog/NewBeginning).

[203]Address by PM Netanyahu at Bar-Ilan University (http://www.mfa.gov.il/MFA/Government/Speeches+by+Israeli+leaders/2009/Address_PM_Netanyahu_Bar-Ilan_University_14-Jun-2009.htm).

[204]Obama's remarks at the UN, September 2011, see: http://graphics8.nytimes.com/packages/pdf/world/Obama-UNGA-Text.pdf

[205]Maariv, Shmuel Rosner, 3.25.2009 (Hebrew).

[206] Laura Rozen first reported in detail what happened in that meeting. See: Revisiting Obama's Riyadh Meeting, Foreign Policy, 7.17.2009.

[207]See: Should Israelis Be Declaring Victory After Today's Summit?, The New Republic, Shmuel Rosner, 9.22.2009.

[208]As Biden Visits, Israel Unveils Plan for New Settlements, New York Times, 3.9.2010.

[209]See: Mutually Assured Distraction, Slate, Shmuel Rosner, 5.23.2011.

[210]2009 Annual Survey of American Jewish Opinion, American Jewish Committee (http://www.ajc.org/site/c.ijITI2PHKoG/b.5472819/k.D6D7/2009_Annual_Survey_of_American_Jewish_Opinion.htm)

[211]This analysis is based on: Jewish opinion: are we suddenly concerned about Obama?, Shmuel Rosner, The Jerusalem Post, 9.30.2009.

[212]Haaretz, Shmuel Rosner, 3.9.2008.

[213]Haaretz, Shmuel Rosner, 2.27.2008 (Obama: I'm a 'stalwart friend' of Israel, its security is 'sacrosanct.')

[214]Haaretz, Shmuel Rosner, 3.2.2007.

[215] Obama to Iran and Israel: 'As President of the United States, I Don't Bluff', The Atlantic, 3.2.2012.

[216]Remarks by the President at Signing of the United States-Israel Enhanced Security Cooperation Act, 7.27.2012 (http://www.whitehouse.gov/photos-and-video/video/2012/07/27/president-obama-signs-us-israel-enhanced-security-cooperation-act#transcript).

[217]Obama Has Been Great for Israel, Colin H. Kahl, Foreign Policy, 8.16.2012.

[218]Prime Minister Netanyahu, AIPAC speech, 5.23.2010.

[219] Jewish Journal, Shmuel Rosner, 9.5.2012.

[220] Jewish Journal, Shmuel Rosner, 9.6.2012.

[221]Jewish Journal, Shmuel Rosner, 6.17.2012.

[222]Jewish Journal, Shmuel Rosner, 8.16.2012.

[223]The following paragraphs draw heavily on my presentation at the third ADL-BESA-CIC International Conference: American-Israeli Relations. Obama or Romney, Israel's Choice, 6.18.2012.

[224]Jewish Journal, Shmuel Rosner, 6.15.2012.

[225]Israeli Public Views on the U.S., 2012, Anti Defamation League, The Begin Sadat Center for Strategic Studies, 6.15.2012.

[226] From the same poll: 60 percent of respondents said they had a "somewhat favorable" or "very favorable" opinion of the president, and just 14 percent said their attitude toward him was unfavorable — but only 32 percent of Israeli respondents "approved of Obama's policies toward Israel, and 21 percent said they disapproved." When it comes to Israeli public opinion, this is a mediocre performance by an American president, at the very least.

[227]Pannels poll, January 2010.

[228] Sixty-eight percent of Israelis said they believe that if Obama is reelected he will "maintain the status quo" in U.S.-Israel relations (8 percent think he'd make it better; 8 percent say he'd make it worse). This might not be bad, had Israelis been happy with the status quo. But they aren't. In 2010, 56 percent of Israelis thought that Netanyahu is "handling the relations" with the United States properly, while only 43 percent said the same about Obama (War and Peace Index, 5.2010).

[229]The February 2012 Israeli Public Opinion Survey, Brookings, 2.29.2012.

[230]This paragraph draws heavily on: Poll Positions, International Herald Tribune, Shmuel Rosner, 3.14.2012.

[231]Jewish Journal, Shmuel Rosner, 7.19.2012.

[232]See Rosner's Domain Iran Trend: Tracking Opinion on Attacking Iran (http://www.jewishjournal.com/rosnersdomain/category/iran_trend).

[233]Jewish Journal, Shmuel Rosner, 8.17.2012.

[234]US: Israel can't destroy Iran's nuclear program, Ynet News, 8.14.2012.

[235]More on this debate: The Things They Stored, International Herald Tribune, Shmuel Rosner, 8.15.2012.

[236]I was in charge of the Israeli component of this survey, and wrote the analysis abut Israel for all involved newspapers. See: International Poll Finds Support Ebbing for U.S. Policy, New York Times, 10.15.2004.

[237]Loving the man with the umbrella, The Guardian, Shmuel Rosner, 15.10.2004.

[238]Among Religious Groups, Jewish Americans Most Strongly Oppose War, Gallup, 2.23.2007.

[239]In these paragraphs I draw heavily on: Haaretz, Shmuel Rosner, 2.4.2007. Similar paragraphs appear in Shtetl, Bagel, Baseball: On the Dreadful Wonderful State of American Jews, Shmuel Rosner, Keter, 2011 (Hebrew).

[240]80% of Americans think Iran's nuclear program threatens the US, Times of Israel, 7.31.2012.

[241]Quotes and content taken from: The Tehran Option, Slate, Shmuel Rosner, 2.27.2007.

[242]The following paragraphs are all based on: **The story of Obama and the 'A' word, Shmuel Rosner, 5.27.2008.**

[243] A long list of Obama's statements on meeting with Iran's leaders, in: On Iran, Parsing Obama, Without Preconditions or Preconceptions, The Atlantic, 5.21.2008.

[244]Fourth Democratic debate transcript:

http://www.nytimes.com/2007/07/24/us/politics/24transcript.html?_r=2&oref=slogin&pag ewanted=all

[245]See: Bush Assails 'Appeasement,' Touching Off Storm, NYT, 5.16.2008.

[246]Bush's Remarks in Israel Rile Obama, NYT, 5.15.2008.

[247]Obama's Metastatic Gaffe, Washington Post, 5.23.2008.

[248]The Obama Learning Curve, WSJ, 5.23.2008.

[249]Haaretz, Shmuel Rosner, 5.17.2007.

[250]The following paragraphs are based on: Jewish Journal, Shmuel Rosner, 8.14.2012.

[251]Romney Seeks Contrast With Obama On Iran In Israel Speech, Bloomberg, 7.30.2012.

[252]2012 AJC Survey of American Jewish Opinion.

[253]Chosen for What? Jewish Values in 2012, PRRI, 4.3.2012.

[254]Peres says Israel can't go it alone in Iran, trusts Obama, Reuters, published in The Jewish Journal, 8.16.2012.

[255]Haaretz, Shmuel Rosner, 6.3.2007.

[256]Renewing American Leadership, Barack Obama, Foreign Affairs, 2007 (http://www.foreignaffairs.com/articles/62636/barack-obama/renewing-american-leadership).

[257]Raising to a New Generation of Global Challenges, Mitt Romney, Foreign Affairs, 2007 (http://www.foreignaffairs.com/articles/62638/mitt-romney/rising-to-a-new-generation-of-global-challenges).

[258]See: The Conversion, Will Saletan, Slate, 8.23.2012.

[259]Workmen's Circle / Arbeter Ring 2012 American Jews' Political Values Survey.

[260]Romney at CBS News, 8.27.2012.

[261]Abortion Will Stay Legal, Romney's Sister Predicts, NYT, 8.29.2012.

[262]See: Romney and Aborion, Glenn Kessler, WP, 9.21.2007.

[263]Jewish Journal, Shmuel Rosner, 4.18.2012 (Care about Iran? You're more likely to vote Romney).

[264]Jewish Journal, Shmuel Rosner, 7.31.2012 (Four lies you've been told about Romney's visit to Israel).

[265]See: What Romney said: Highlights from Haaretz's interview with Obama's adversary, 7.27.2012.

[266]Jewish Journal, Shmuel Rosner, 7.29.2012 (Romney in Israel, The real story).

[267] Netanyahu wants 'clear red line' to avoid Iran war, AFP, 9.3.2012.

[268]Dark Horse, Kenneth D. Ackerman, 2003, page 164.

[269]Romney: 'I like being able to fire people who provide services to me,' Washington Post, 1.9.2012.

[270]See: GOP: Obama's 'You Didn't Build That' Will Take Us to November, Sunshine State News, 8.30.2012.